The Book of Healing Symbols for Animals

Written by Sarah Berrisford
Reiki Master Teacher

Copyright 2024

Please refer to the index at the rear of this book to find page numbers for specific symbols.

Introduction

The symbols in this book have been channelled whilst working with animals. I use these symbols alongside Reiki treatments, but you can use them within any healing session. You can also use the symbols on yourself to become familiar with them.

Before using a particular symbol on an animal, practice drawing it in the air. Feel the best way to draw the symbol, sometimes I use my finger, or whole hand/ palm and sometimes I draw the symbol in my mind's eye – there is no right or wrong way, allow your intuition to guide you as to what feels right for the specific situation.

Before using a symbol, it is a good idea to centre yourself, so that you can work intuitively. If you already practice a healing method or meditation, then you will likely have your preferred way to do this. If not, then here are some simple instructions you could follow:

1) Take 3 deep breaths, in through your nose and out through your mouth. Be aware of how your breath enters and fills your body and be aware of how you exhale slowly through your mouth.
2) Feel your feet connected to the ground, be aware of the soles of your feet. Feel the pressure evenly through your feet to the ground.
3) You may like to place your hand(s) on your heart, feel your heart beat and as you exhale, think of slowing your heartbeat and relaxing your body.
4) Place a hand(s) on your solar plexus/ stomach area, becoming aware of any fizzing or anxious feeling and as you exhale think of calming this area, both internally and externally.
5) Allow your mind to clear from outside thoughts and distractions. If any thoughts of everyday life come to mind, just acknowledge them, and allow them to pass, they are not needed right now.
6) Think of your body and energy being open and connected to all around you, with an inner calmness and peace resonating from your very core.
7) Feel your heart beat a strong yet gentle beat that is unaffected by outside influence, it just carries on pulsating in rhythm.
8) Then, when you are ready draw the desired symbol on to the animal. Generally, the symbol is drawn in the animal's energy field/ aura and then you can push the symbol into the body to the amount that feels right.

The symbols in this book should be used alongside proper veterinary care. If your animal is sick or hurt, take him to the vet and then use the symbols to promote healing.

When working with the symbols, I use the symbol for the symptom at least once a day, whether that be in person or distantly.

Once the symbol has been drawn and I have guided the symbol into the animal, I stay present with the symbol and animal (or meditate visualising the symbol) for a minimum of 5 minutes, but often longer.

Each symbol in this book has been channelled for its initial use and then re-used over and over again, which in turn, increases its power and intent.

When using the symbols, we still need to listen to our intuition, for instance, I used the skin condition symbol on three different horses with mud fever. All three horses had received the same vet care including topical creams and antibiotics over the course of two months, to no avail. Within one week of using the symbols, there was an improvement in two of the horses and it looked to be quite miraculous how to all just cleared up. However, the third horse showed no improvement. I sat with the horse and the symbol and allowed my mind to become still yet open. In my mind I could see what you could describe as a 'waking dream' where something was being added to the horses feed. I then heard the words 'heal from the inside out' and then 'herbs' and finally 'echinacea.' This horse then received an echinacea tincture in her feed and the mud fever started to clear. So, sometimes it's not about physically healing the issue, but facilitating a space to help us to see what will aid the issue.

You will notice throughout the book that some symbols may have a specific place on the body that I would recommend drawing them. With others just do what feels right. Don't worry about getting things wrong. If you're not sure where to draw the symbol, you could draw it in lots of places and see where it feels right or comfortable to draw it the most and then perhaps come back to that place each day to redraw.

<u>Abnormal Growth/ Tumour</u>

Any abnormal mass of tissue or swelling. Like a cyst, a tumour can form in any part of the body. A tumour can be benign or cancerous (malignant)

Drawing instructions for symbol to help with an abnormal growth

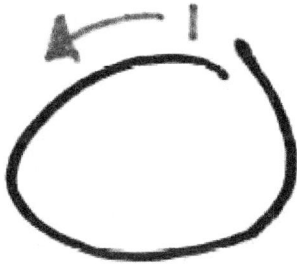

Abscess

An abscess is a painful collection of pus, usually caused by a bacterial infection.

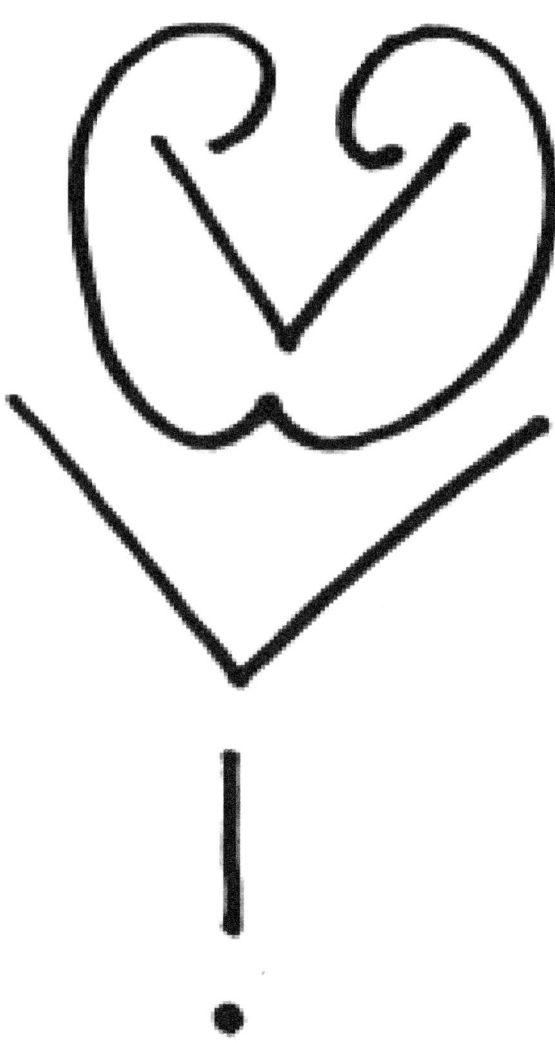

Drawing instructions for a symbol to help with an abscess:

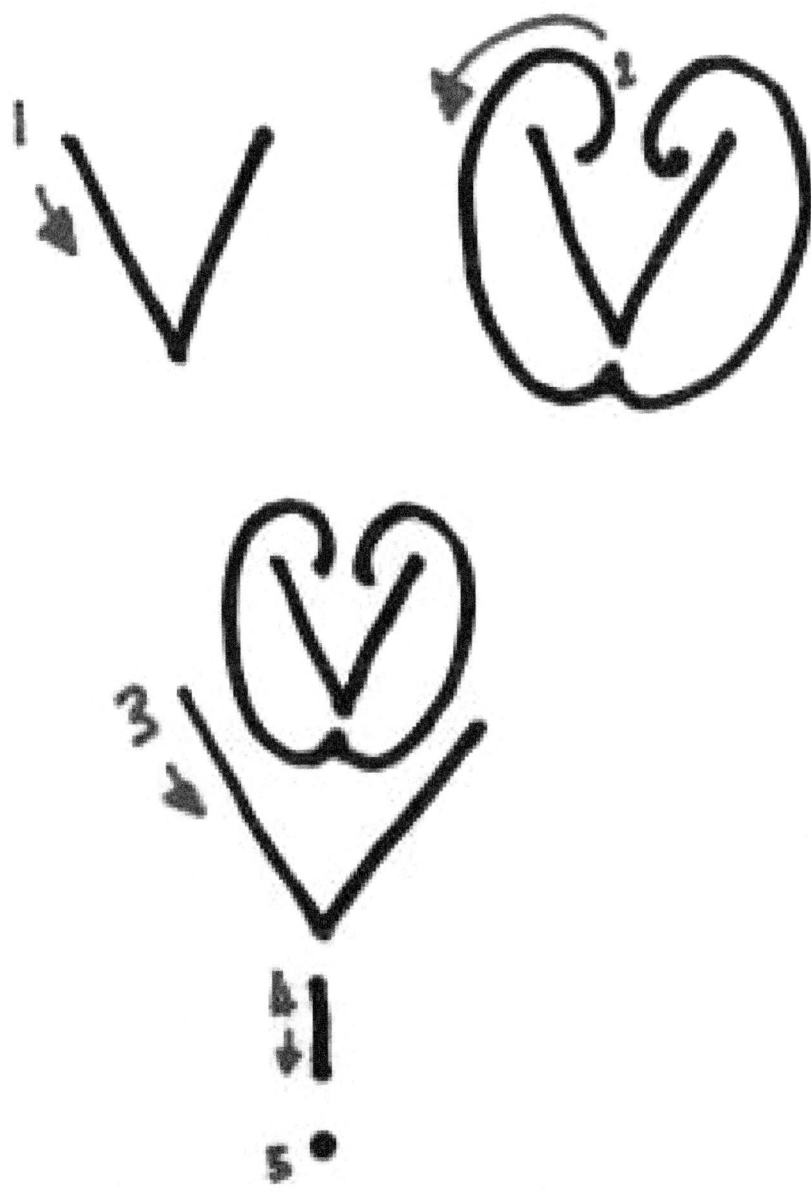

Allergies

Allergies are caused by the immune system mistaking a harmless substance for something harmful. Common triggers include pollen, food and chemicals.

This symbol can be drawn anywhere on the body. If you are not sure where to draw it, then choose the place where allergies are apparent.

Ne aware that although we may draw the symbol in a 2D format you may find that the circles move in a vortex or spin around the centre line as the symbol enters the animal's body. Just allow the symbol to be as it needs to be, for that specific animal or situation.

The more that you work with the different symbols, the more that you will find that they take on a life of their own/ do their own thing as they connect to the animal's energy.

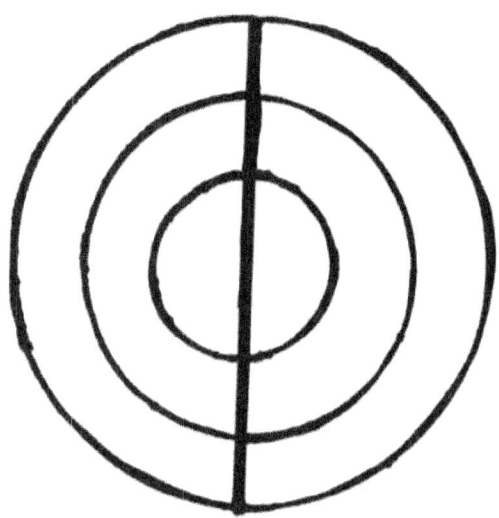

Drawing Instructions for a symbol to help with allergies:

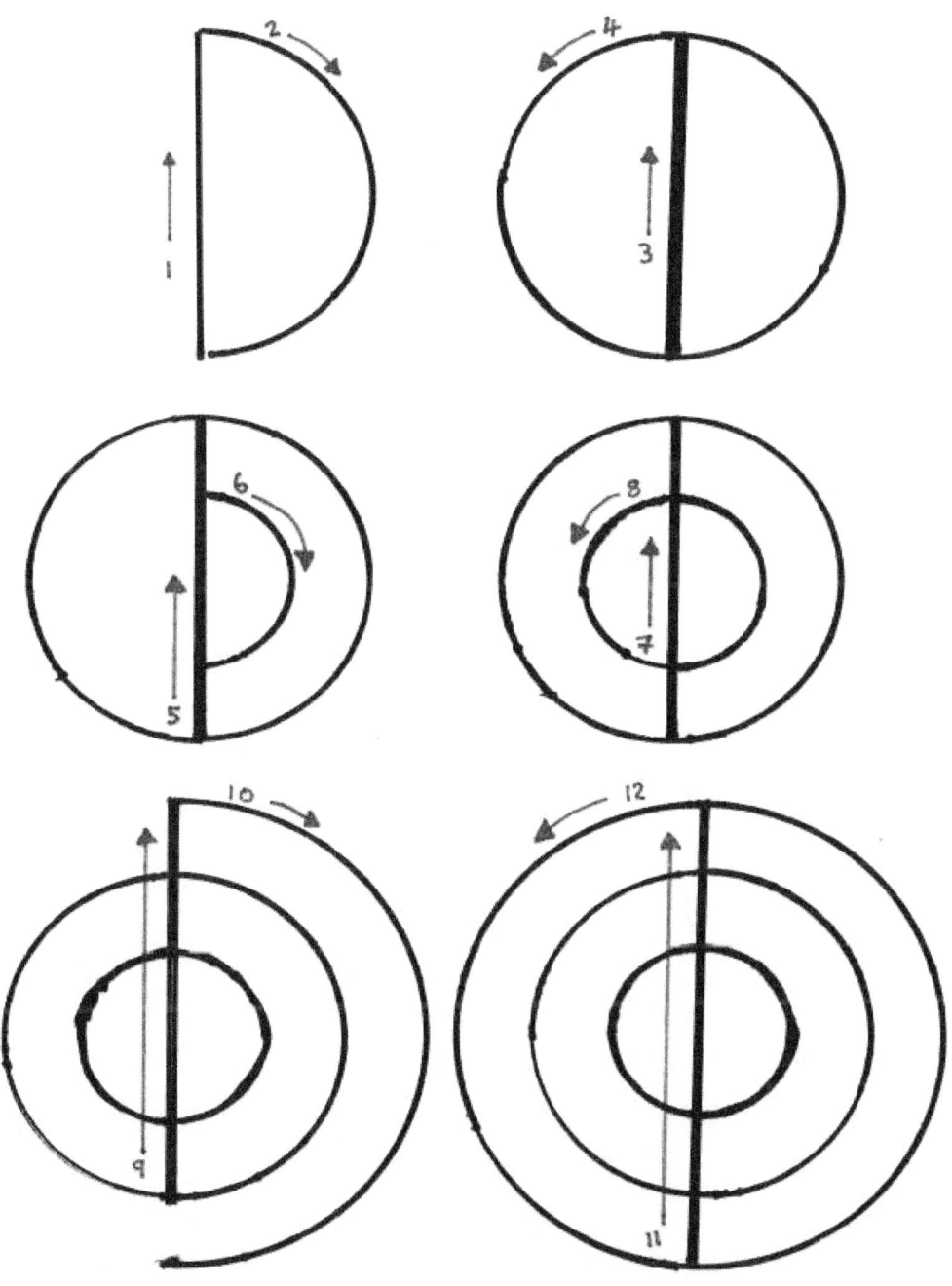

Anxiety

Anxiety is a feeling of unease, such as worry or fear, that can be mild or severe. It causes increased alertness, fear, and physical signs.

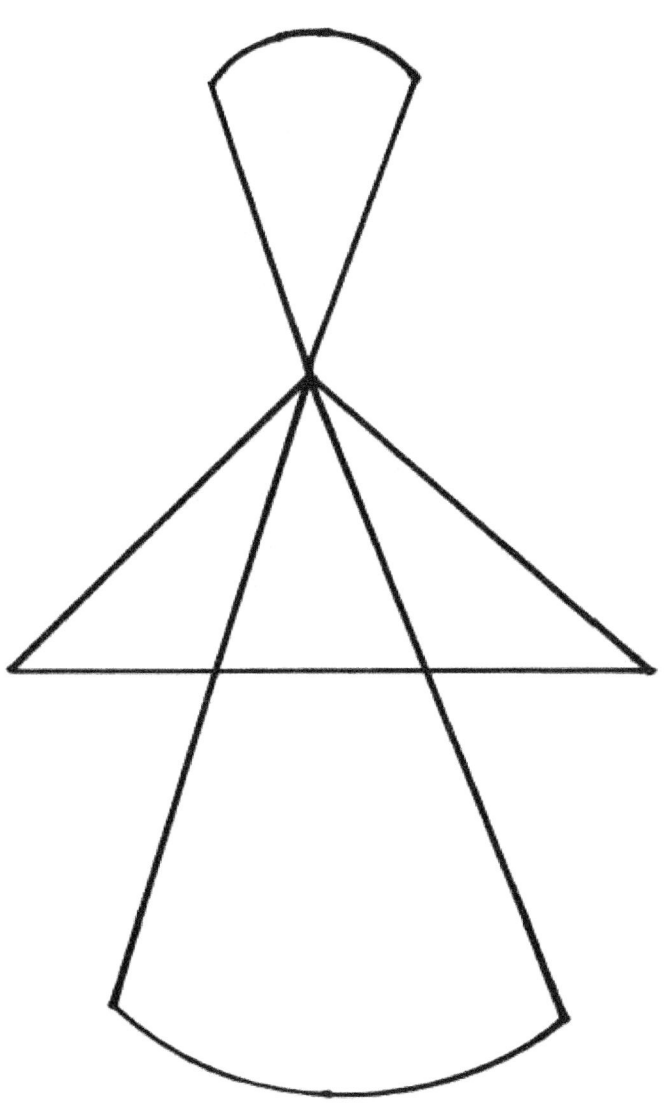

Drawing instructions for a symbol to help with anxiety:

The centre triangle is drawn over the heart area of the animal or person. The top loop is drawn around the head and the bottom loop is drawn around the stomach and bowel. This symbol links the heart, mind and gut. The symbol finishes in its centre where it begins.

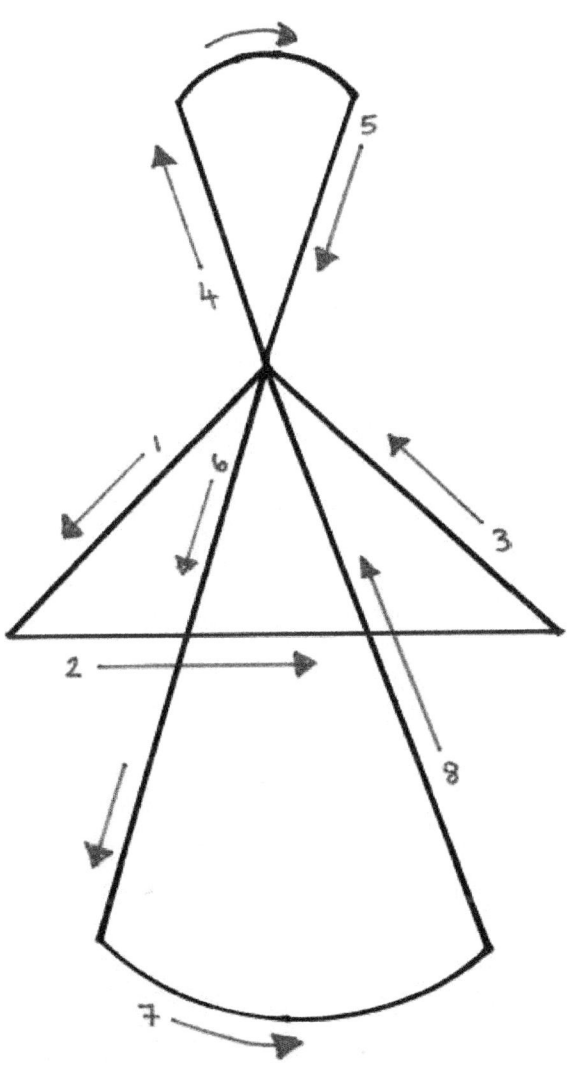

Appetite (balance)

The appetite serves to regulate adequate energy intake to maintain metabolic needs.

Drawing instructions for a symbol to help with balancing the appetite (lack of or too much):

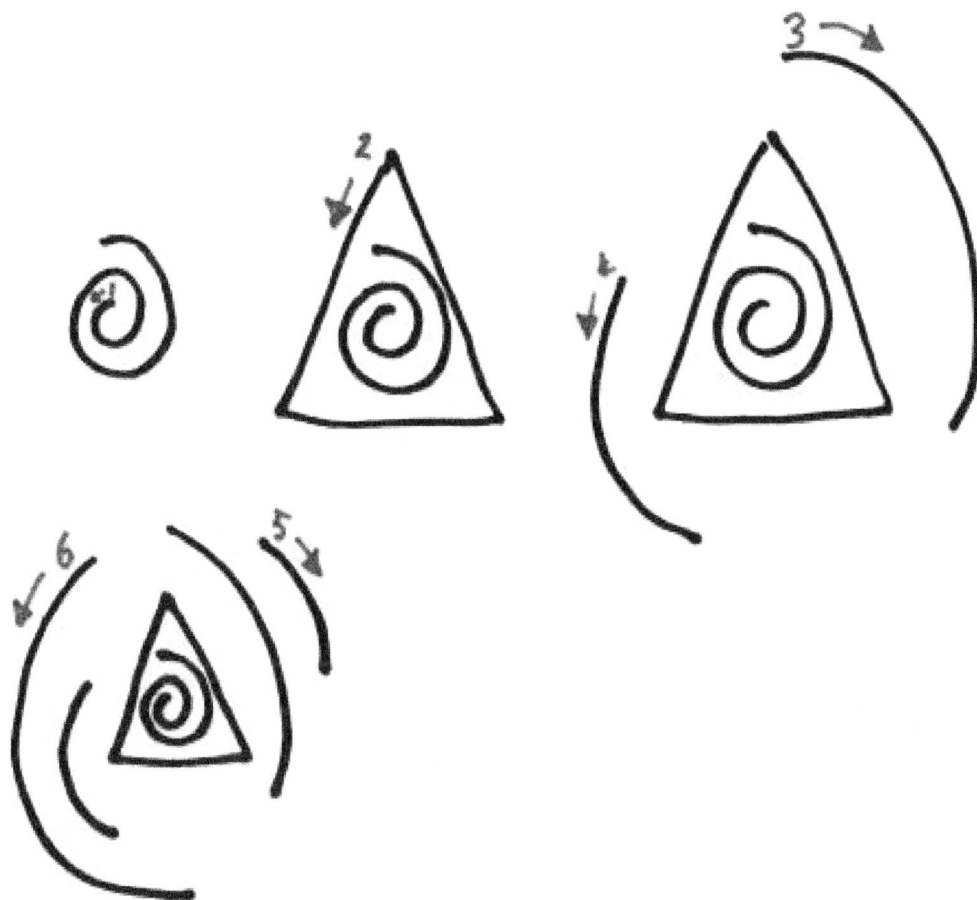

Arthritis

Arthritis is a common condition that causes pain and swelling (inflammation) in the joints.

I tend to use this symbol over the whole animal, not just the area that is problematic area, but follow your intuition.

The first three circles that are drawn on the lines of the triangle have their starting point anywhere on the outside of the triangle.

The final two circles (numbers 7 and 8) have their starting point at the top of each circle.

Drawing Instructions for a symbol to help with arthritis:

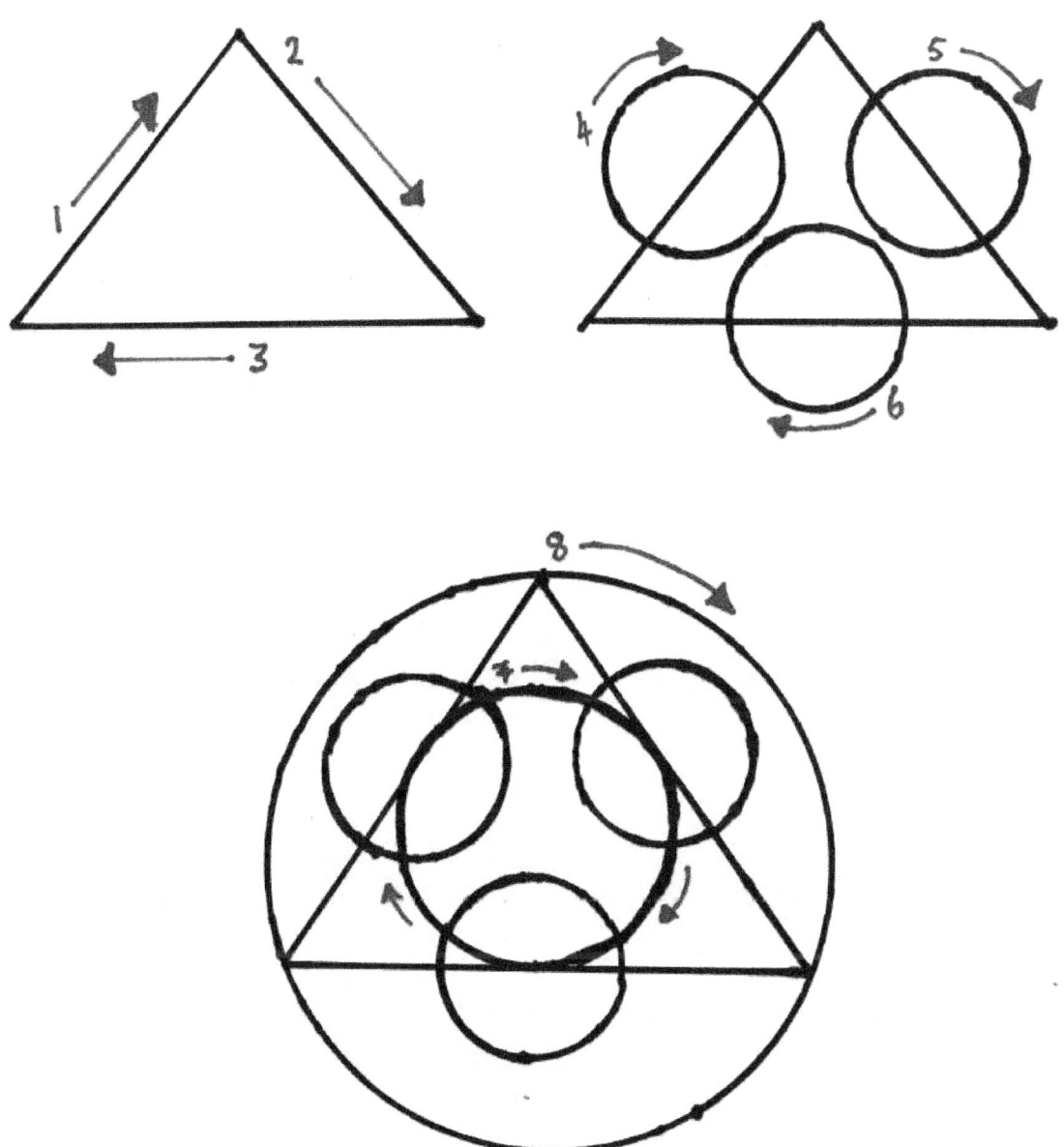

Back issues

Drawing instructions for a symbol to help with back issues:

Line 1 can be drawn along the spine (if possible)

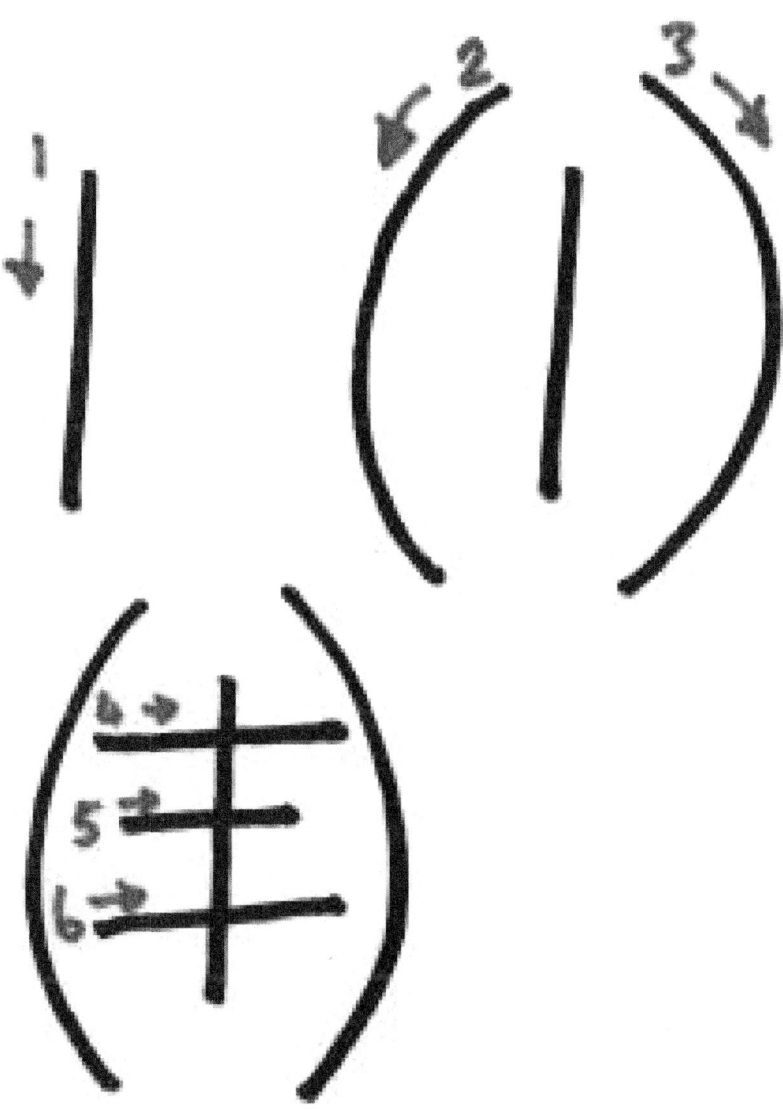

Back pain

Back pain can have many causes. It is not always obvious what the cause is. Often it gets better on its own. A common cause of back pain is an injury like a pulled muscle (strain) or sometimes, medical conditions like a slipped disc or sciatica.

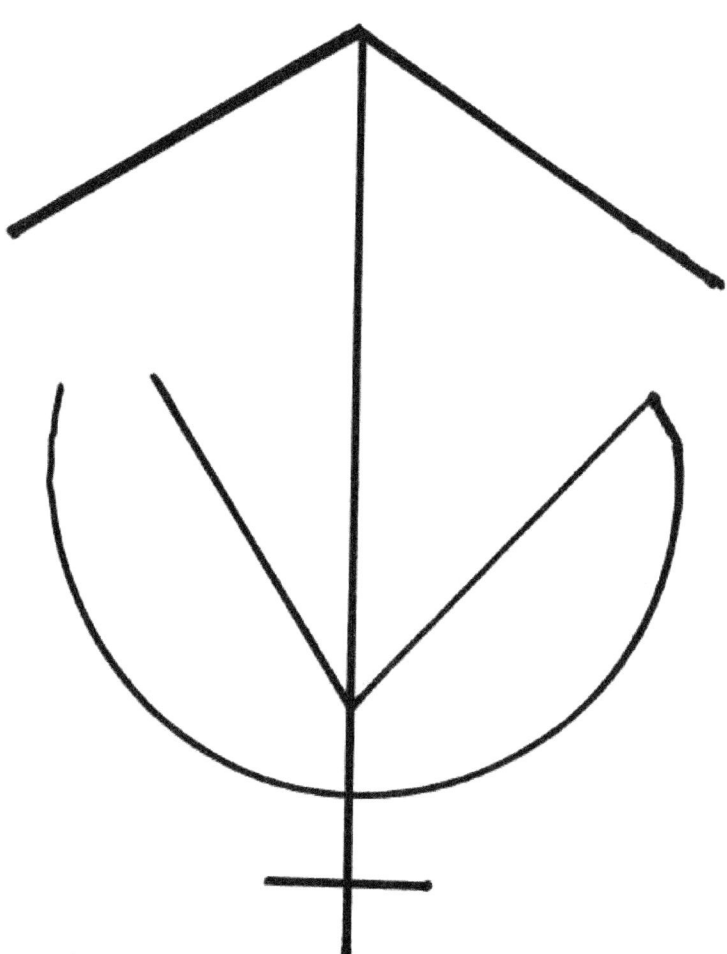

Drawing instructions for a symbol to aid with back pain:

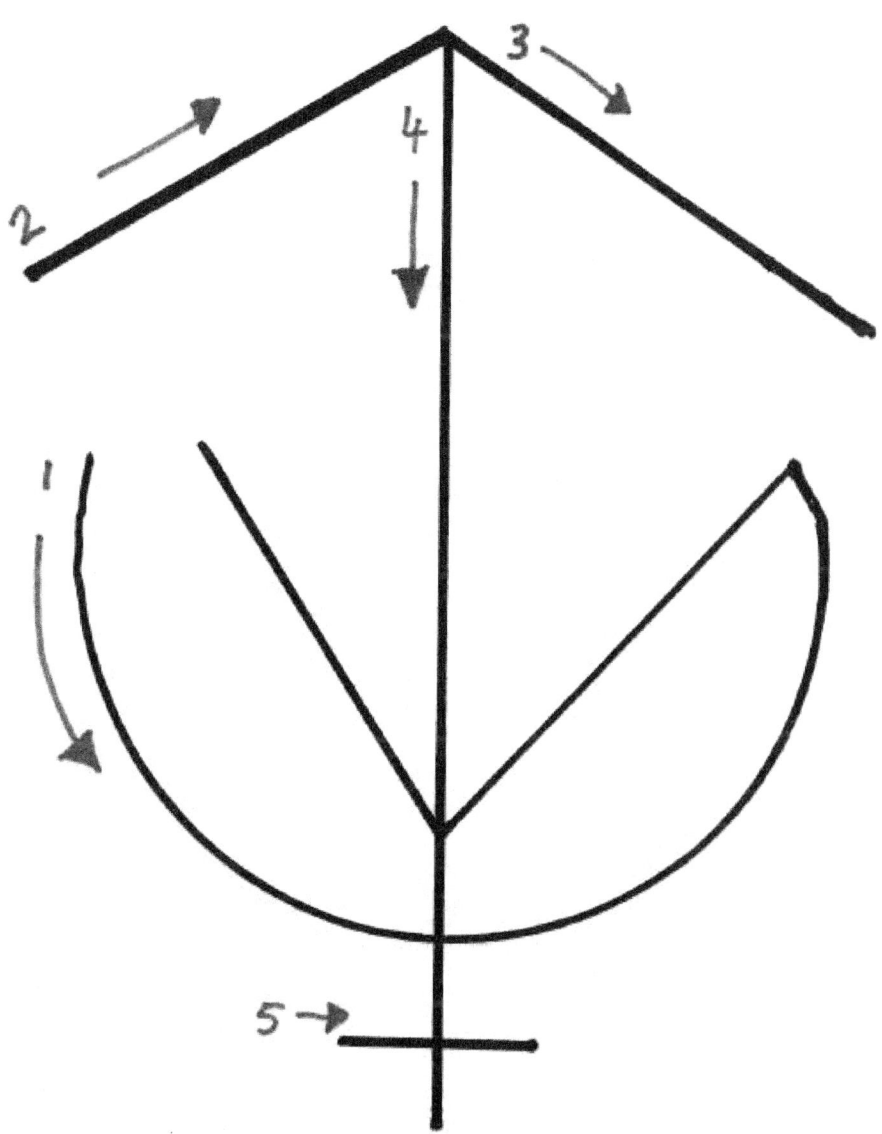

Blindness / Loss of sight – coping emotionally and physically

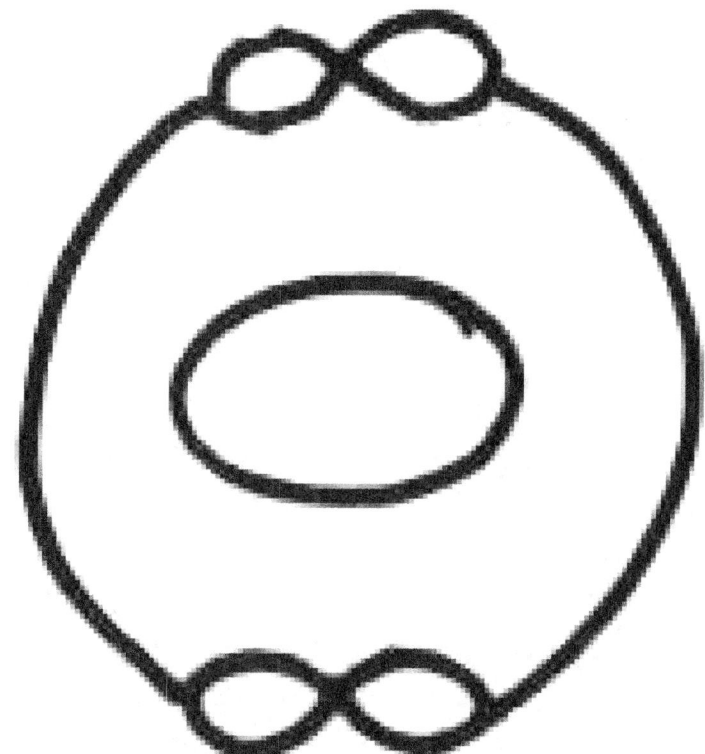

Drawing instructions for a symbol to help with the demands of loss of sight.

The 1st oval is drawn over the eye area. Lines 2 and 3 are drawn over the aura.

Bloat

Bloat occurs when a dog's stomach fills with gas, food, or fluid and subsequently twists.

Drawing instructions for a symbol to help with bloat:

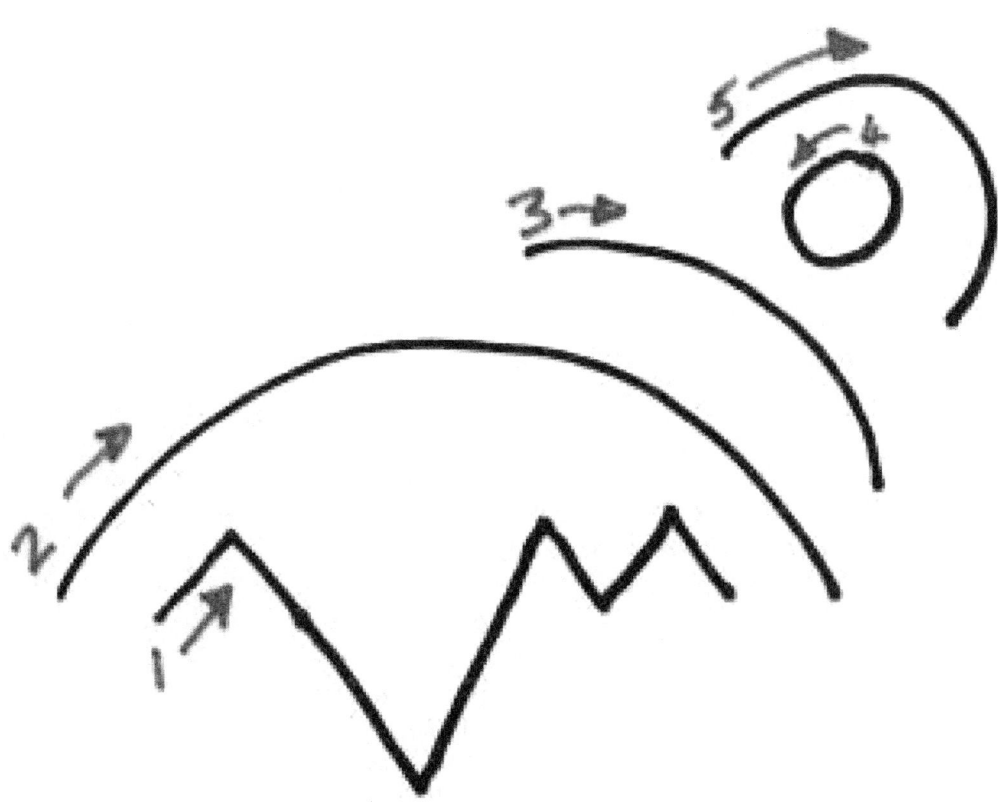

Broken/ Fractured Bones

Broken bones can happen after an accident like a fall, or being hit by an object. Most broken bones are treated with a cast, splint, or brace. It is very important that they are seen to by a vet asap.

Common types of fractures include:

- Stable fracture. The broken ends of the bone line up and are barely out of place.
- Open (compound) fracture. The skin may be pierced by the bone or by a blow that breaks the skin at the time of the fracture. The bone may or may not be visible in the wound.
- Transverse fracture. This type of fracture has a horizontal fracture line.
- Oblique fracture. This type of fracture has an angled pattern.
- Comminuted fracture. In this type of fracture, the bone shatters into three or more pieces.

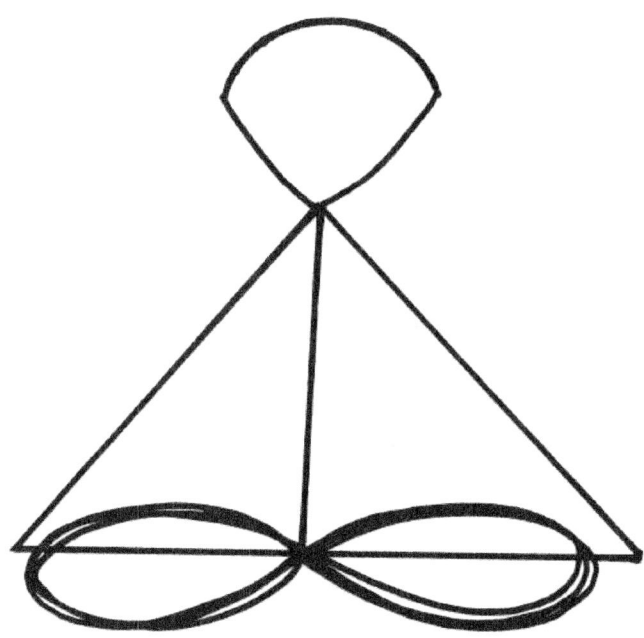

Drawing instructions for a symbol to help with bone injuries:

I draw this symbol over the break or fracture. The infinity symbol at the base of the triangle is drawn three times.

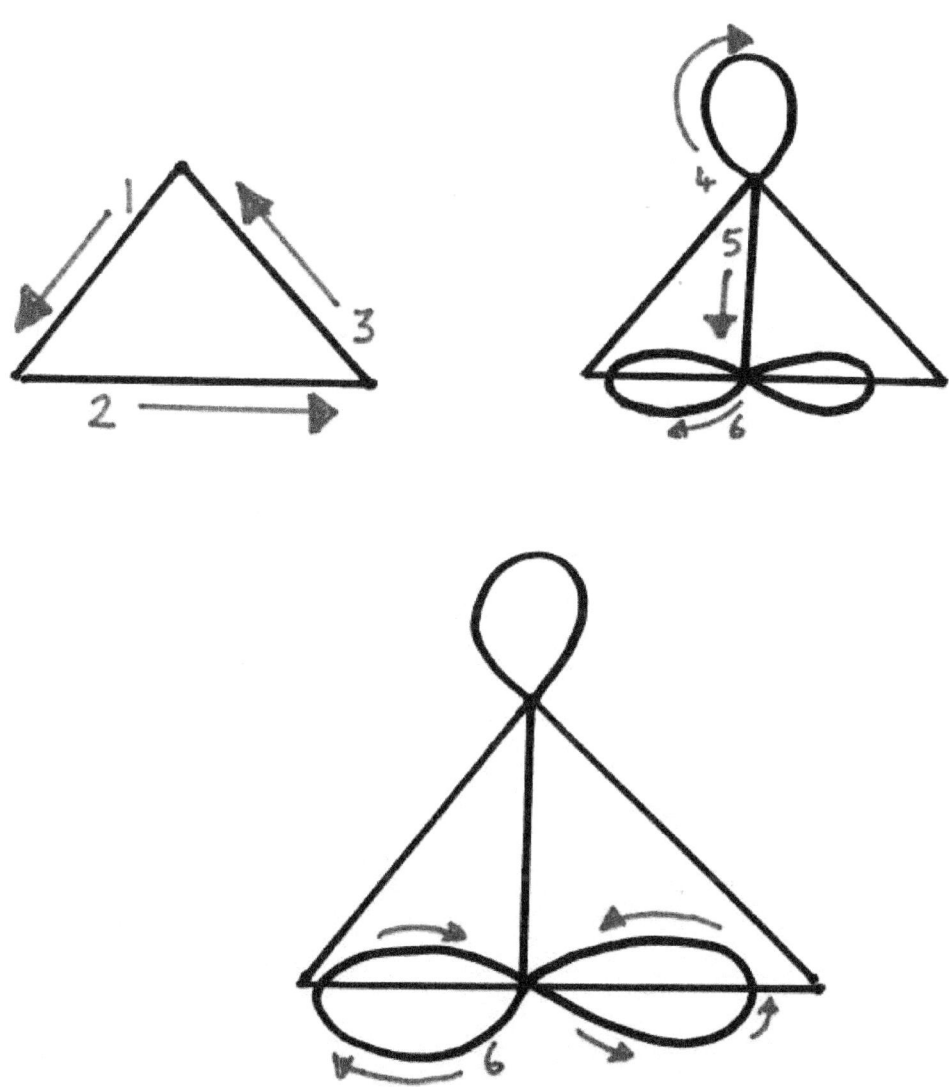

Chakras:

Crown Chakra

The crown chakra is tied to inner wisdom. When out of balance it could influence depression and disconnection from the outside world.

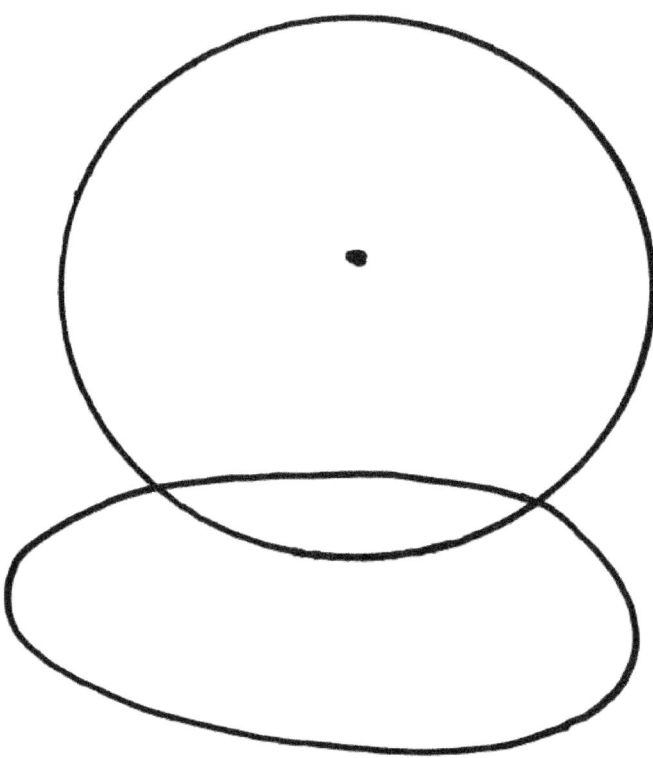

Drawing instructions for Crown Chakra Symbol:

The first circle is drawn around the circumference of the head (where you would measure to fit a helmet). The second circle is drawn around the crown chakra. The final 'dot' is held in place for at least 10 seconds to empower the Crown Chakra.

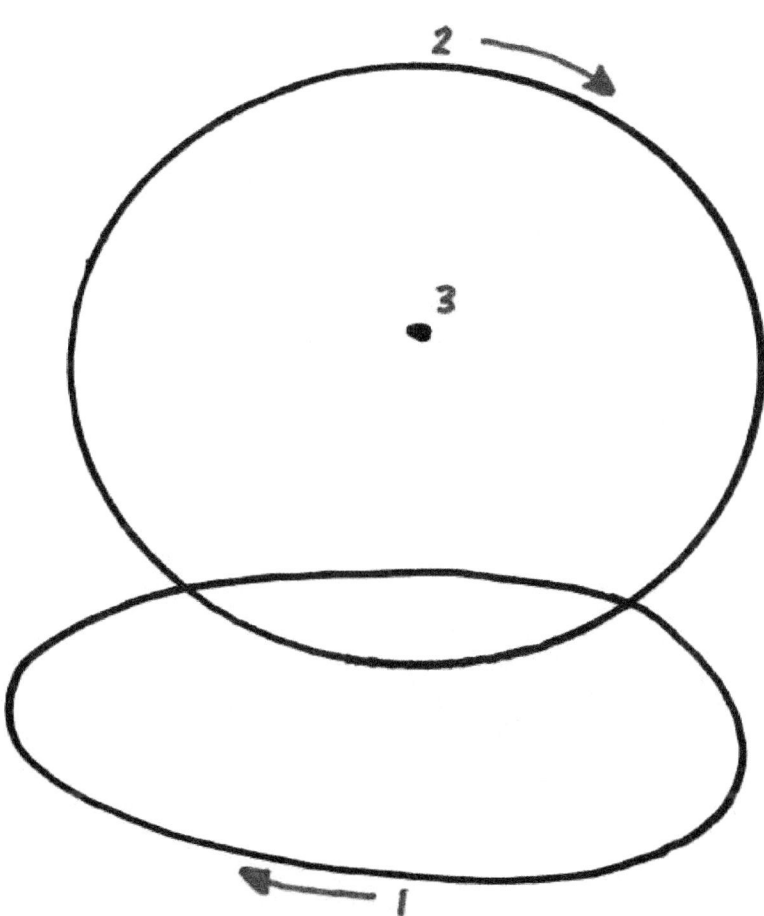

Third Eye Chakra

The third eye controls intellect and intuition. When it is out of balance, a headache or dizziness can occur.

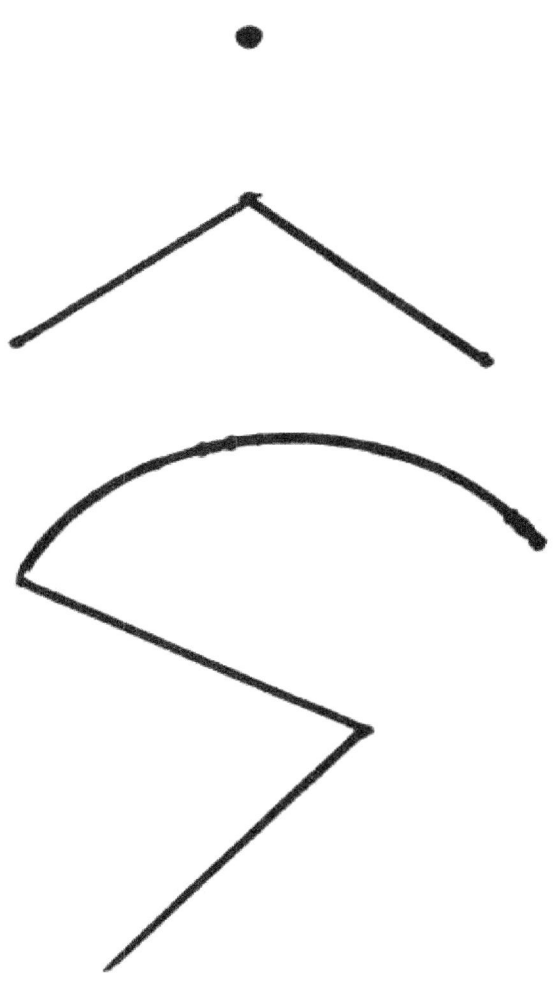

Drawing instructions for Third Eye Chakra Symbol:

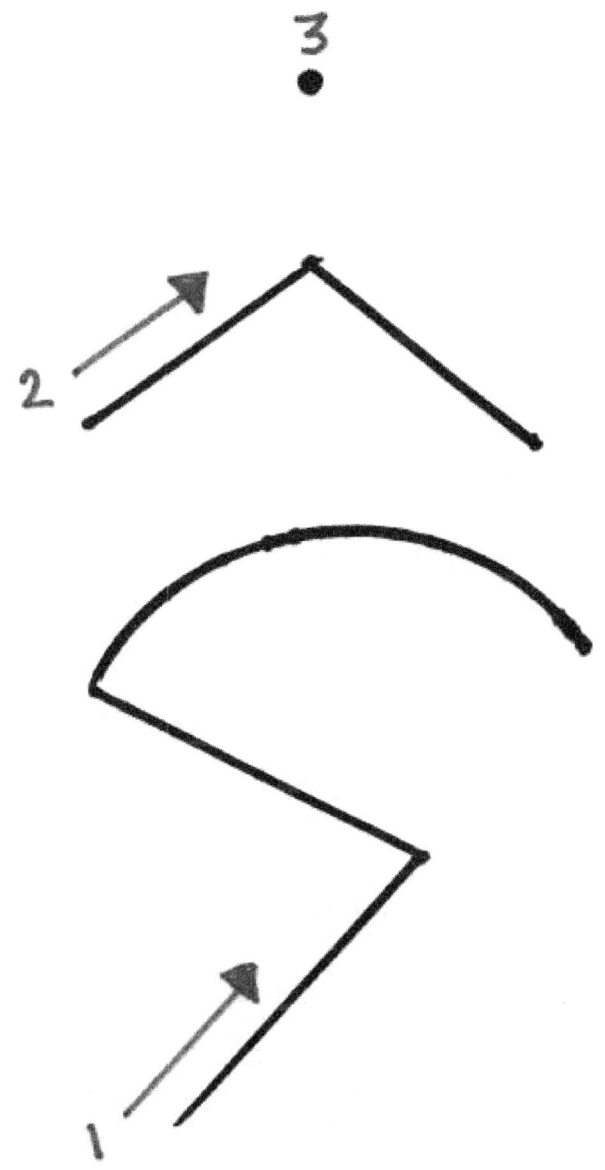

Throat Chakra

The throat chakra is tied to communication, both listening and self-expression

Drawing instructions for Throat Chakra Symbol:

The first figure of 8 (upright infinity symbol), is to aid communication for the animal to feel listened to and heard.

The second figure of 8 (horizontal infinity symbol) is to aid listening and understanding of others.

Both figure of 8's start from the centre point.

Heart Chakra

The heart chakra is linked to self-love and love for others. Being able to give and receive love, unconditionally.

When this chakra is out of balance it can cause lack of trust, jealousy, anxiety, and fear.

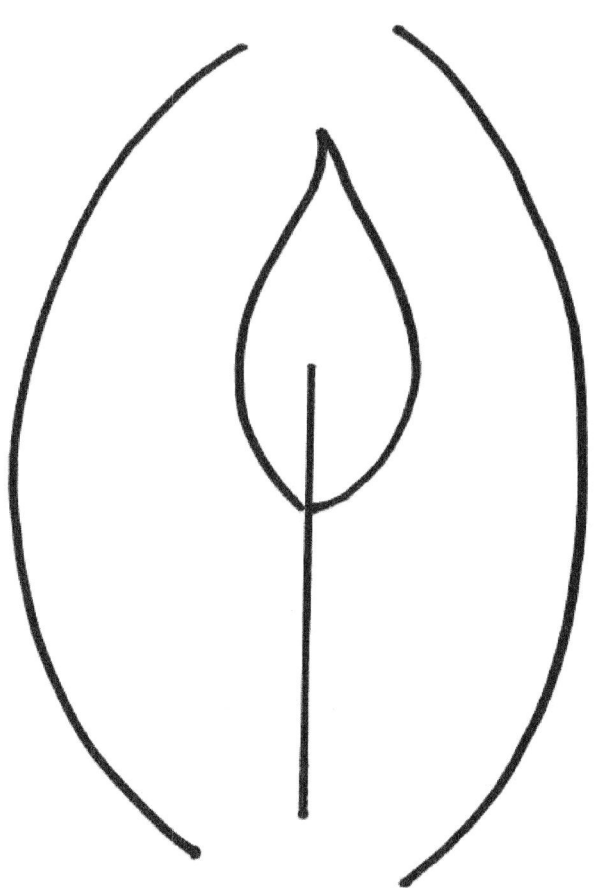

Drawing instructions for Heart Chakra Symbol:

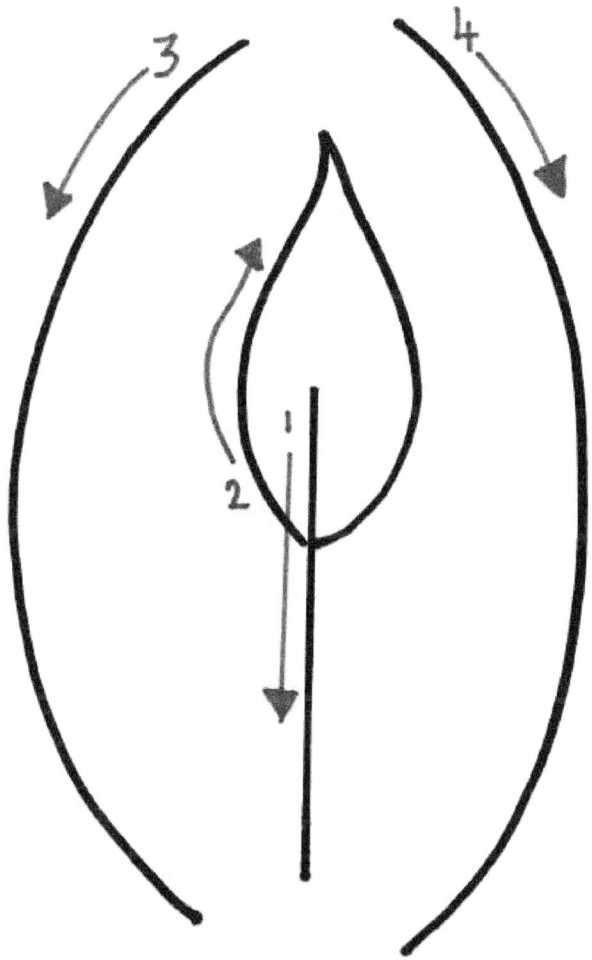

Solar Plexus Chakra

This chakra is the centre of the self-esteem and the emotions such as, ego and aggression. When this chakra is out of balance, physical symptoms can occur e.g. digestive problems.

When this chakra is imbalance, it produces self-confidence and energy.

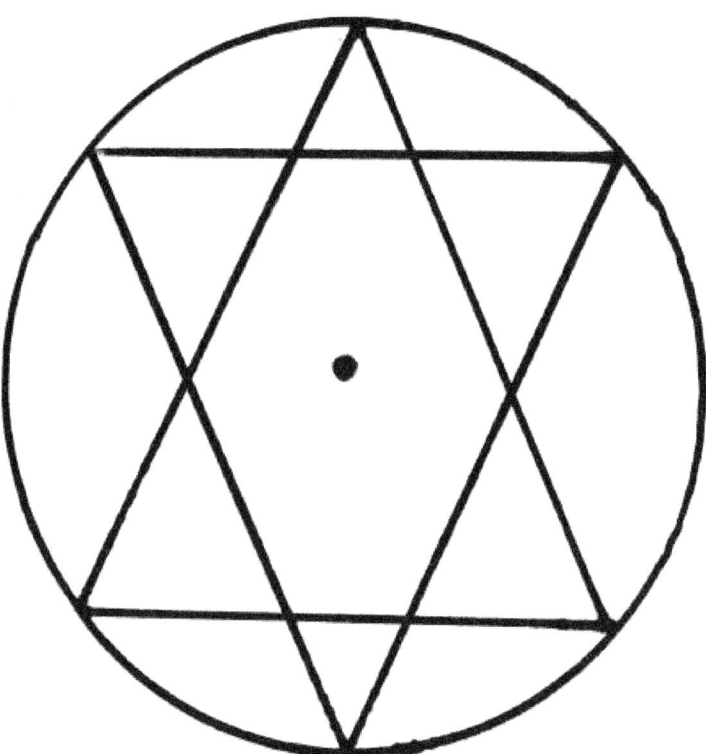

Drawing instructions for Solar Plexus Chakra Symbol:

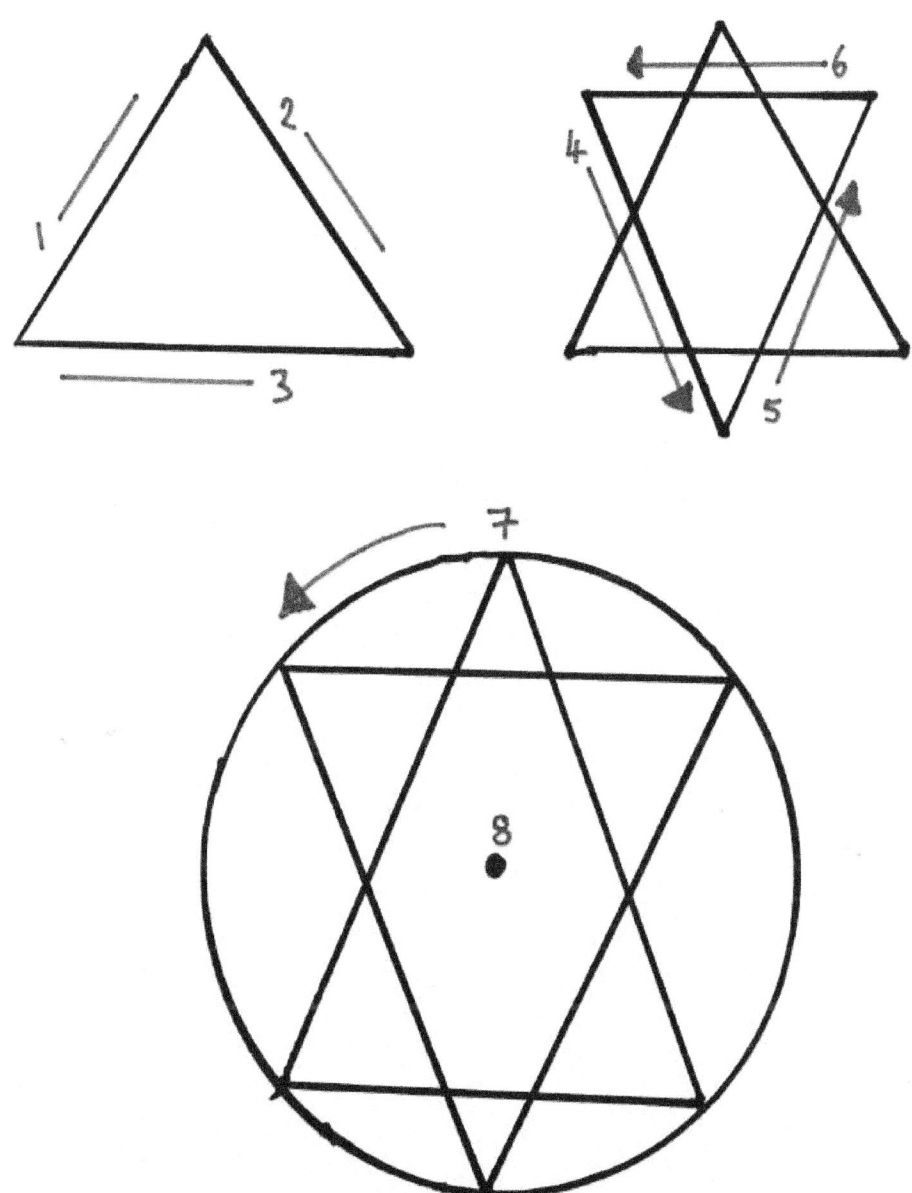

Sacral Chakra

The Sacral Chakra is related to sexuality, compassion, self-worth, and creativity. When this chakra is out of balance it can cause emotional out bursts, sexual issues and a lack of creativity

Drawing instructions for Sacral Chakra Symbol

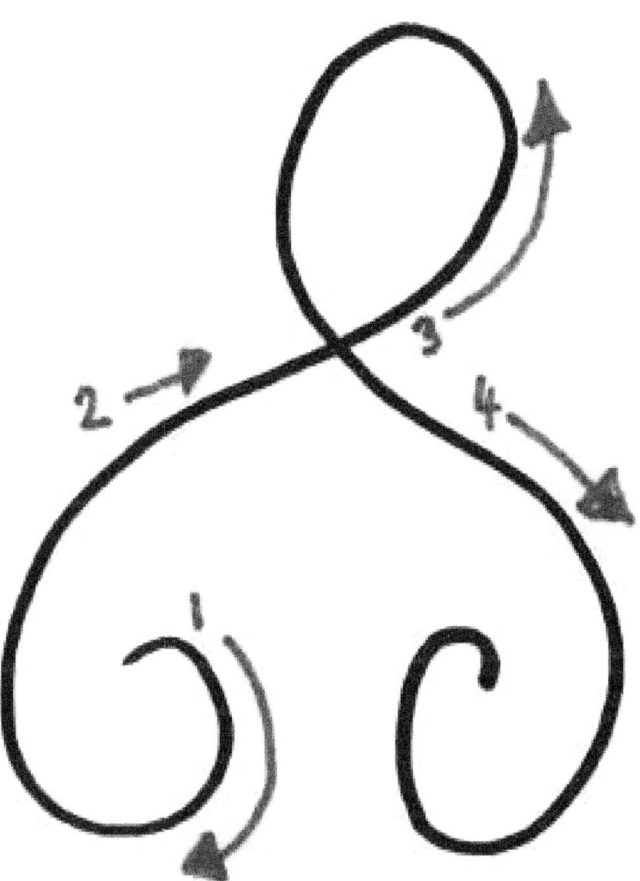

Root Chakra

The root chakra controls the feelings of security, survival, ambition, dependency, and stability. When unbalanced, it can lead to feelings of deep fear and insecurity.

When the root chakra is in balance, it creates feelings of security, positivity, energy, strength and independence.

Drawing instructions for Root Chakra Symbol:

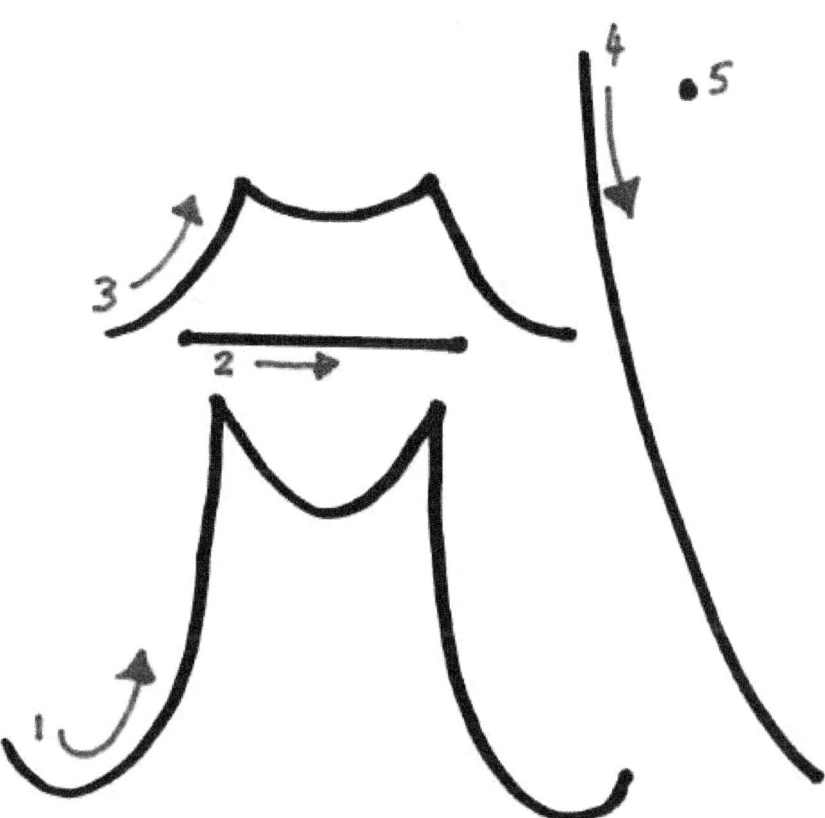

Chest issues

Drawing instructions for a symbol to help with chest issues:

Chewing (Excessive)

When an animal is showing behaviours of chewing or destroying his surroundings

Drawing instructions for a symbol to help relive the underlying symptoms causing excessive chewing:

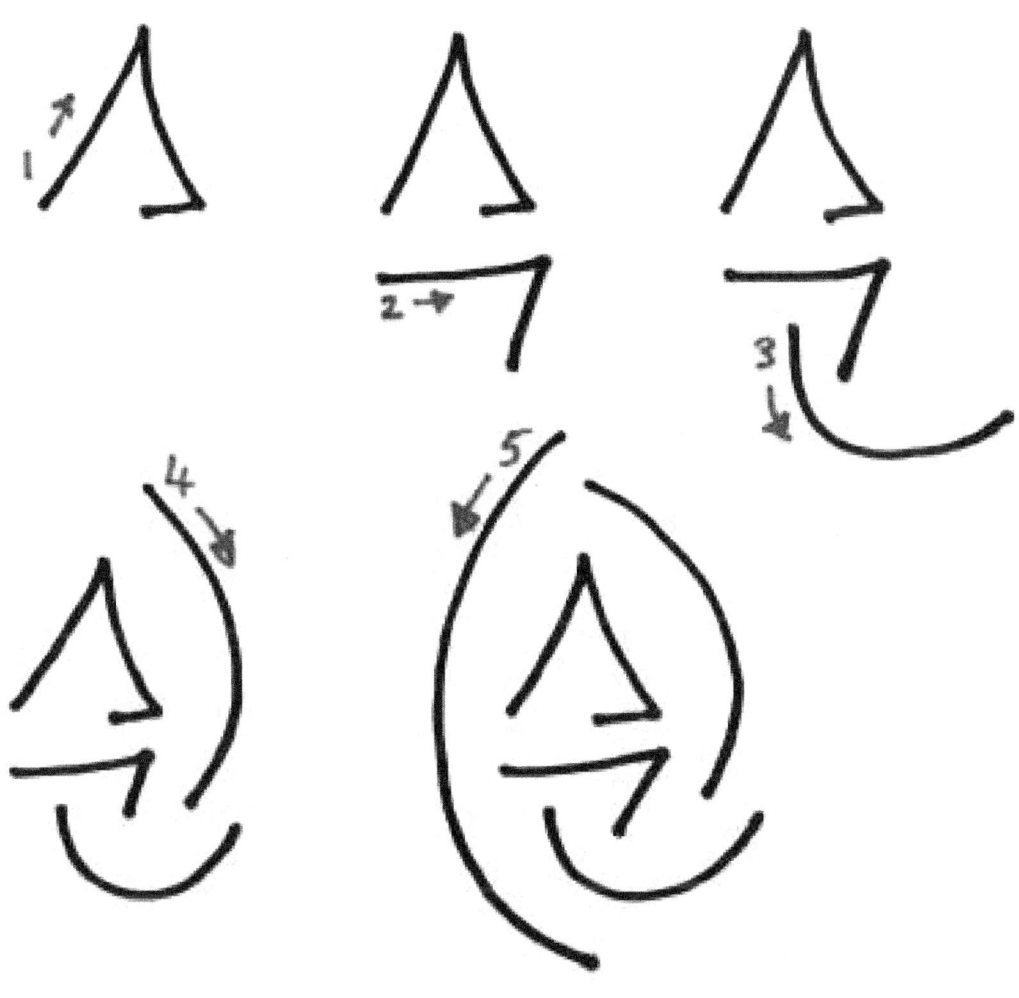

Circulation

The movement of blood through the vessels of the body, which is induced by the heart pumping.

Drawing instructions for a symbol to help with circulation:

Colic

Cramps or a dull ache in the abdomen.

Drawing Instructions for a symbol to help with colic symptoms:

This symbol is drawn 3D. The first line is drawn on the aura. The second zigzag line, comes down from the aura towards the body. The third spiral is drawn from its centre, over the area that is causing pain, for example, the stomach/ intestines.

Common Cold

An infection of the nose and throat. Colds are caused by viruses. Symptoms of a cold include a blocked or runny nose, a sore throat and coughing.

Drawing instructions for a symbol to help the symptoms of the common cold:

COPD / Breathing

Chronic obstructive pulmonary disease (COPD) is the name for a group of lung conditions that cause breathing difficulties.

Drawing instructions for a symbol to help with COPD:

If possible, start with line 1 tracing down the windpipe and draw the triangle over the lung area.

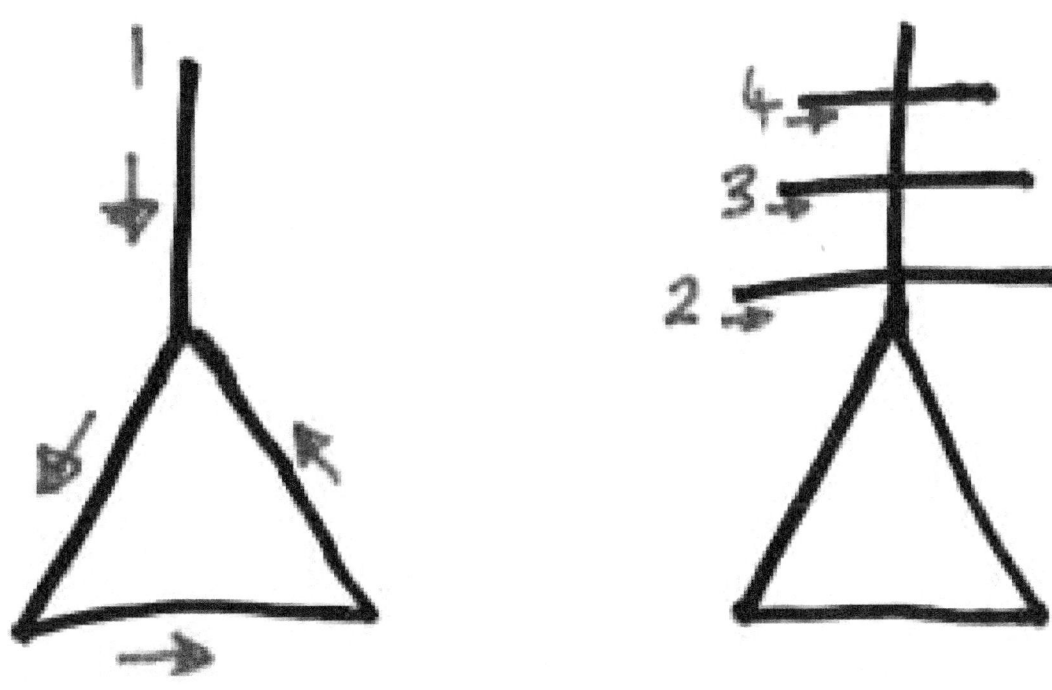

Cough

Coughing is an important reflex that helps protect the airways and lungs against irritants. Occasional coughing is normal, but a persistent cough or one that is accompanied by other symptoms might be a sign of a more serious condition.

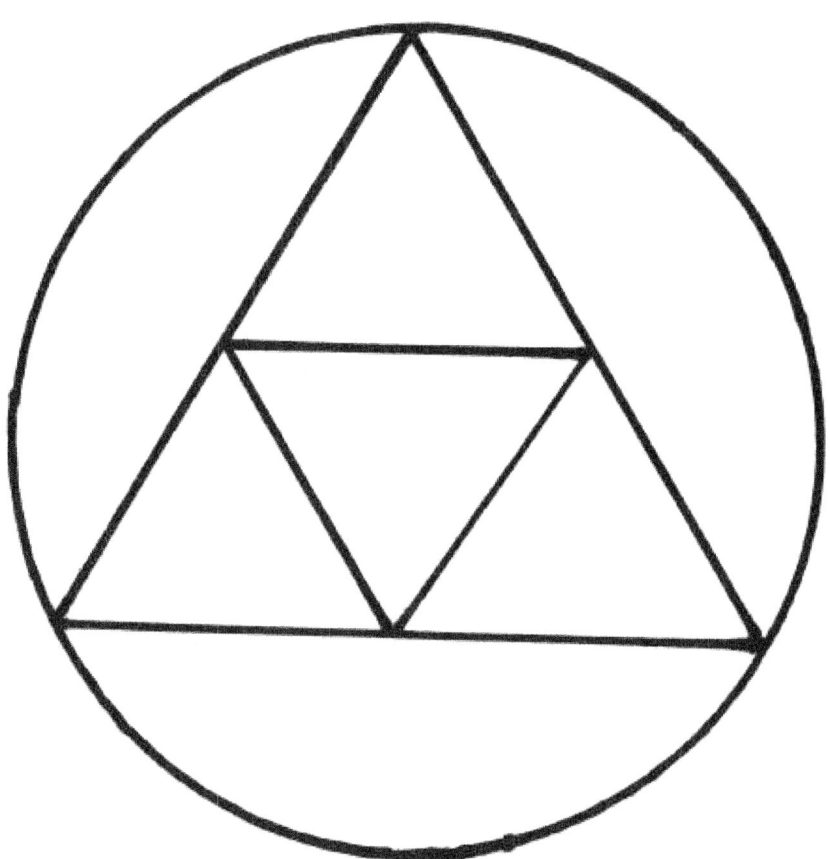

Drawing Instructions for a symbol to help with cough issues:

The bottom left triangle is drawn first, followed by the bottom right, and then the top triangle. Finally the circle is drawn around the outside of the traingles.

Once the symbol is complete, you may find that the 'upside down triangle' in the centre, draws out the cough/ energy, filtering it into light as it passes through.

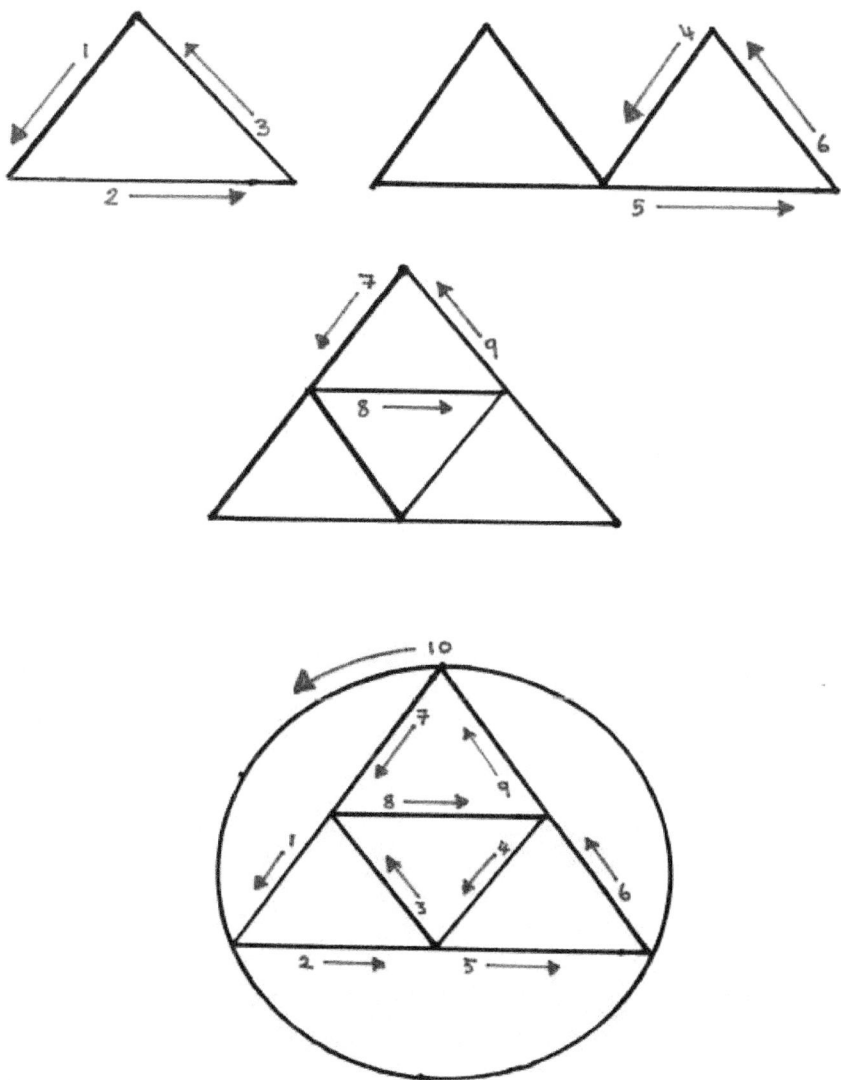

53

Cribbing / Windsucking

Cribbing or crib biting is a behaviour in which the horse grabs onto a fixed object with the front teeth and arches their neck, whilst using their mouth to suck air into the cranial oesophagus, making a grunting noise.

Windsucking is similar but the horse achieves the same position without grabbing a fixed object.

Drawing instructions for a symbol to help with cribbing and windsucking:

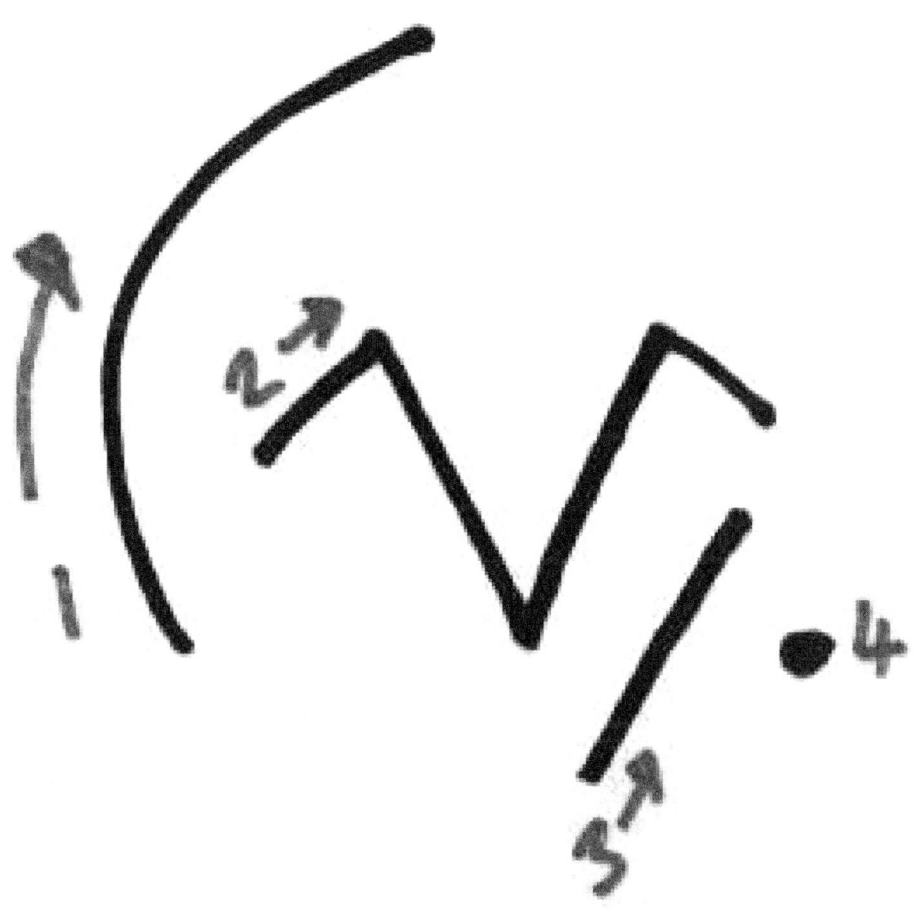

Cyst

A sac that may be filled with fluid, air, or other material. A cyst can form in any part of the body, including bones, soft tissues and organs. Most cysts are noncancerous (benign), but sometimes cancer can cause a cyst.

Drawing instructions for a symbol to help reduce cyst(s)

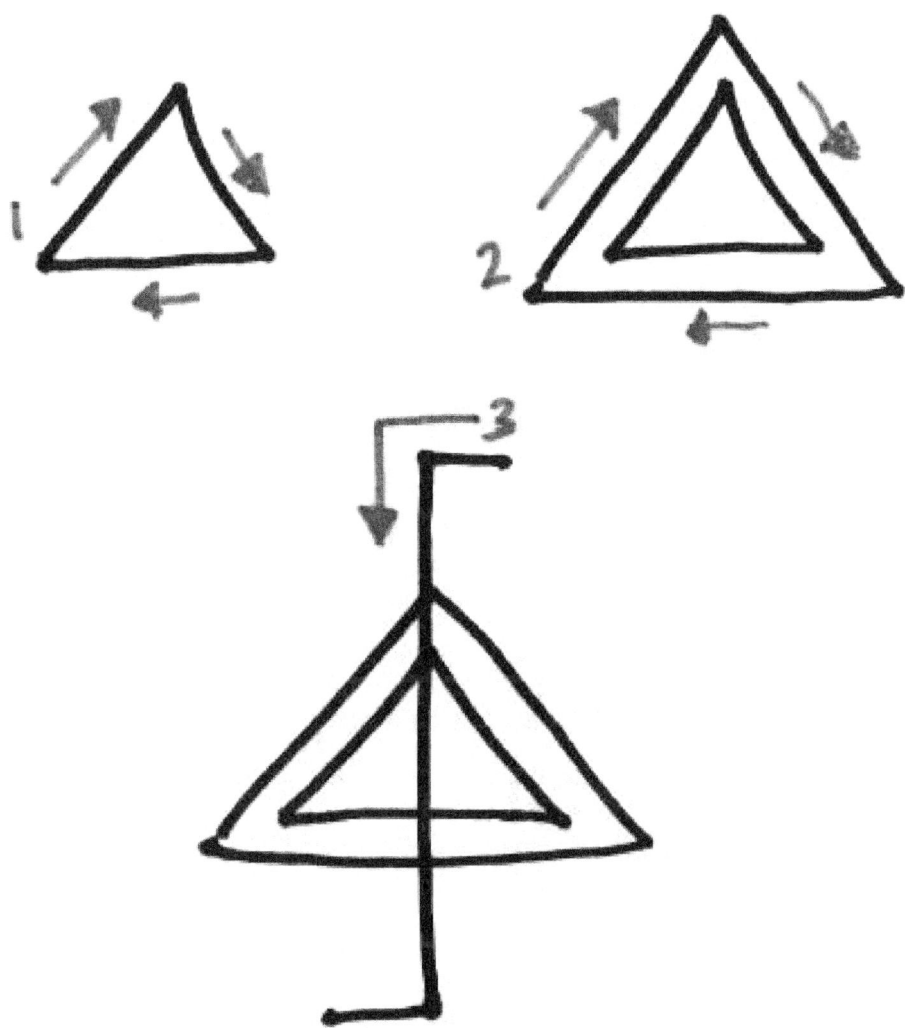

Dehydration

Dehydration is caused by not drinking enough fluid or by losing more fluid than you take in. Fluid is lost through sweat, vomiting, urine or diarrhoea. The severity of dehydration can depend on a number of factors, such as level of physical activity, climate and diet.

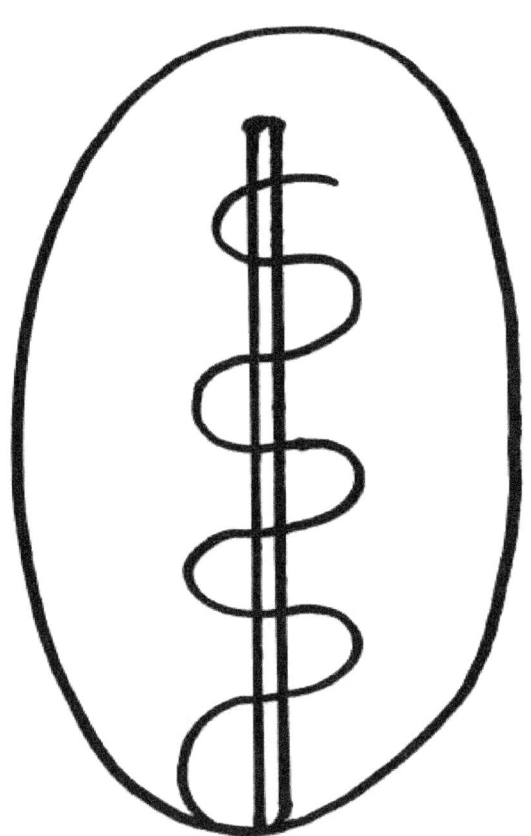

Drawing instructions for a symbol to help with cause and effect of dehydration:

   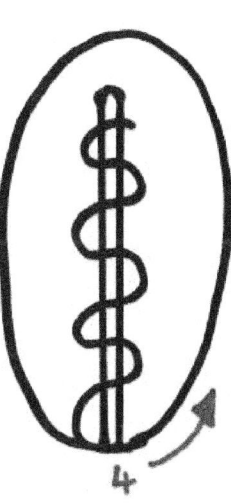

Depression

Depression causes a persistent feeling of sadness and loss of interest. It affects how you feel, think and behave and can lead to a variety of emotional and physical problems

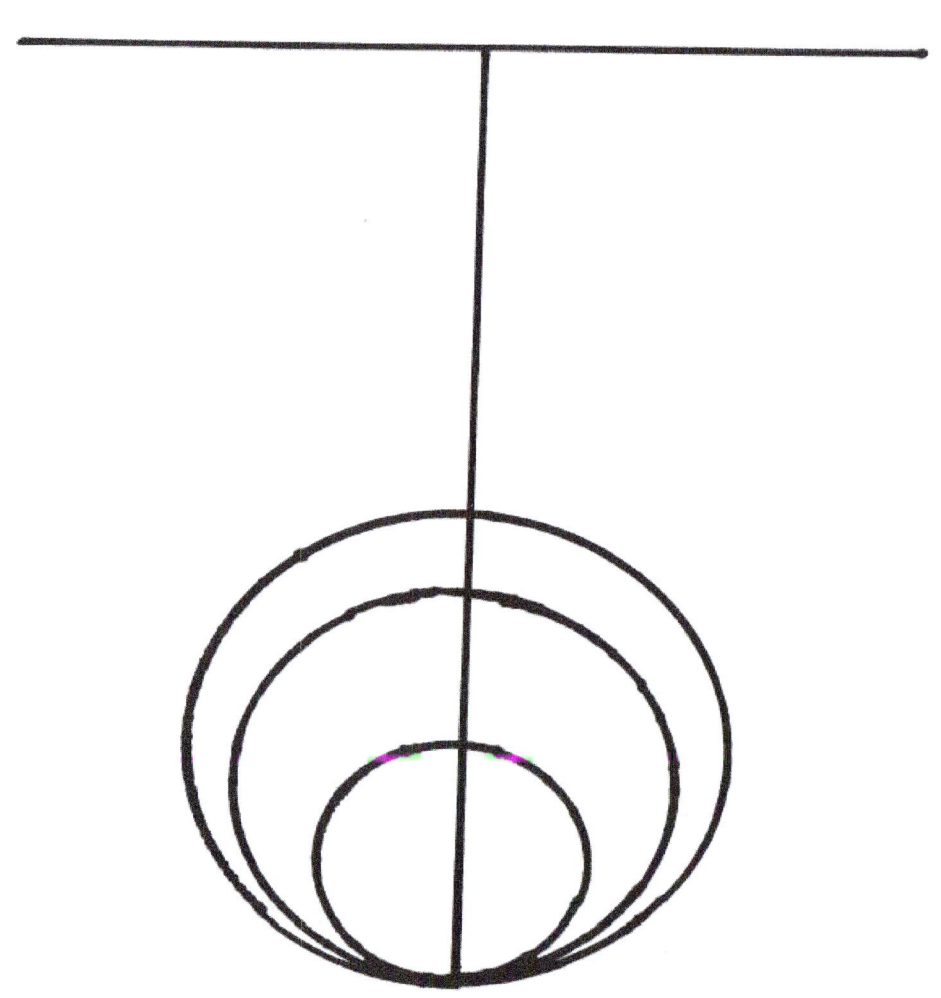

Drawing instructions for a symbol to aid with depression:

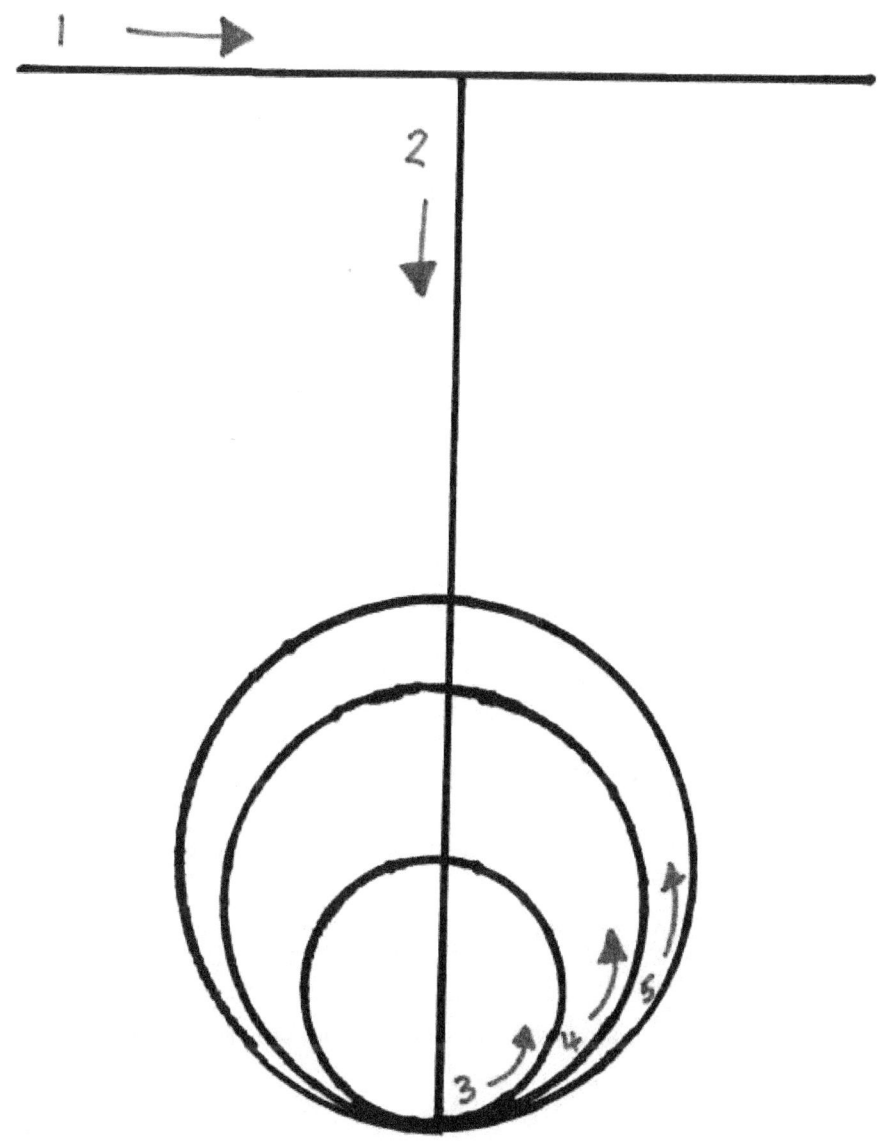

Diabetes

Diabetes is a chronic disease that occurs either when the pancreas does not produce enough insulin or when the body cannot effectively use the insulin it produces.

Drawing instructions for a symbol to help with diabetes:

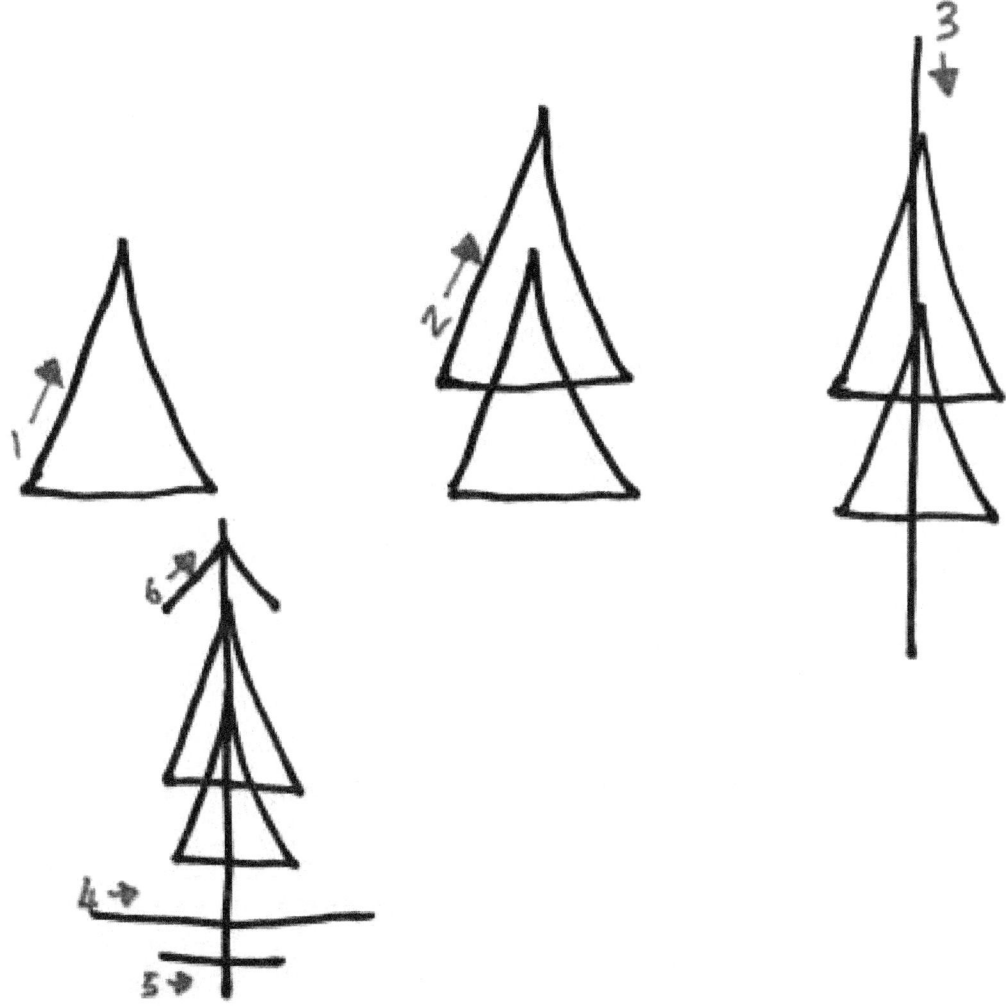

Diarrhoea

Diarrhoea is passing looser, watery or more frequent stools, than is normal for the animal.

Drawing instructions for a symbol to help with the symptoms of diarrhoea:

Digestive Issues

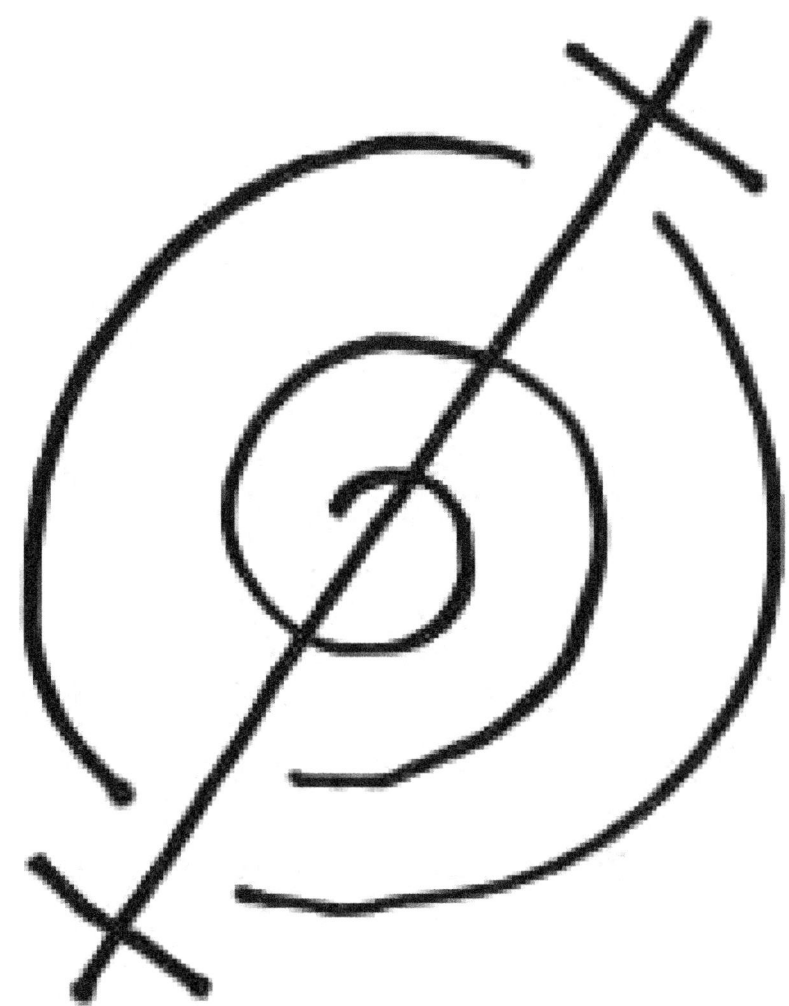

Drawing instructions for a symbol to help with digestive issues:

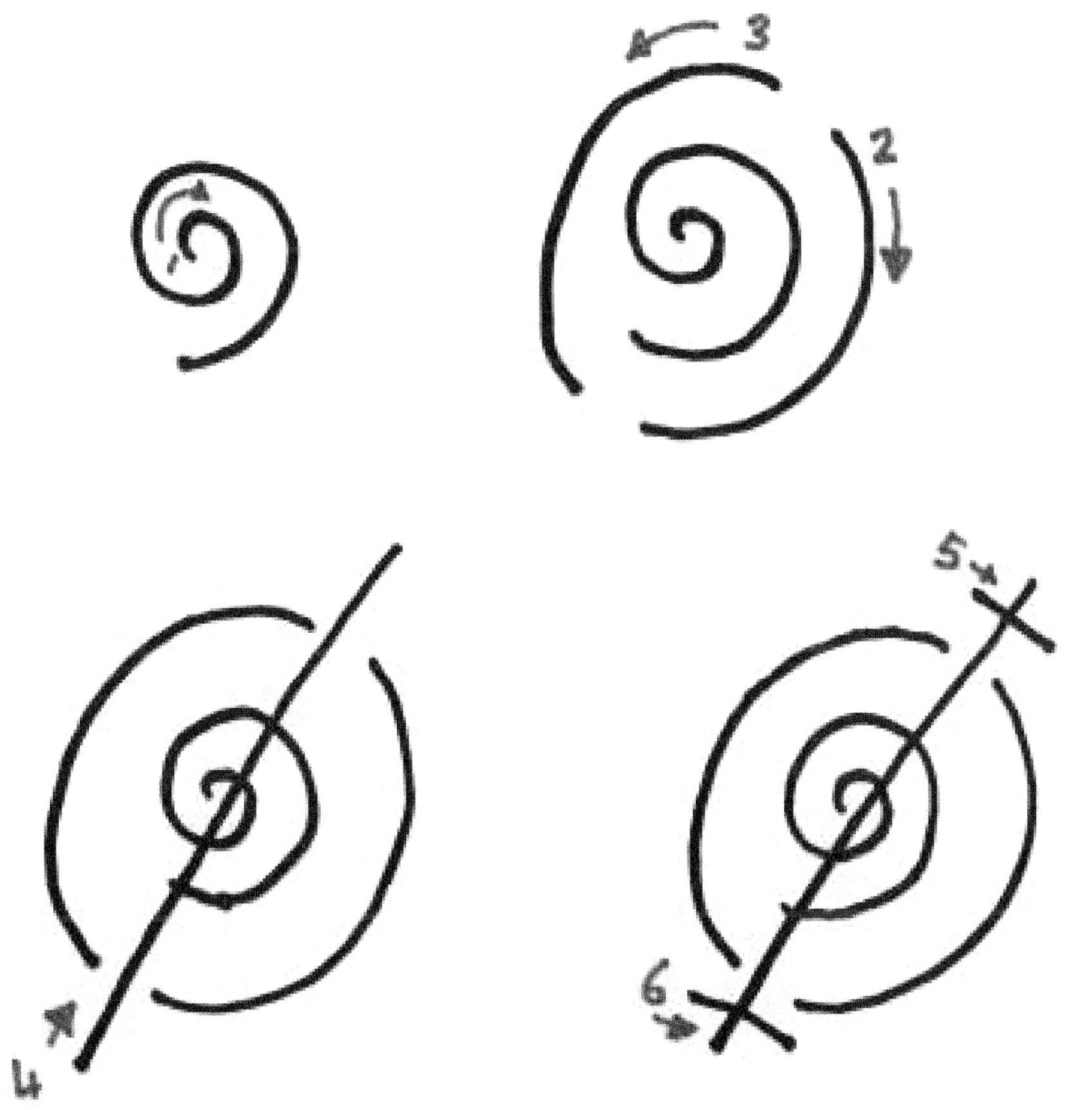

Ear Issues

There are many issues that can affect the ears, from hearing problems to infections.

Drawing instructions for a symbol to help with ear issues:

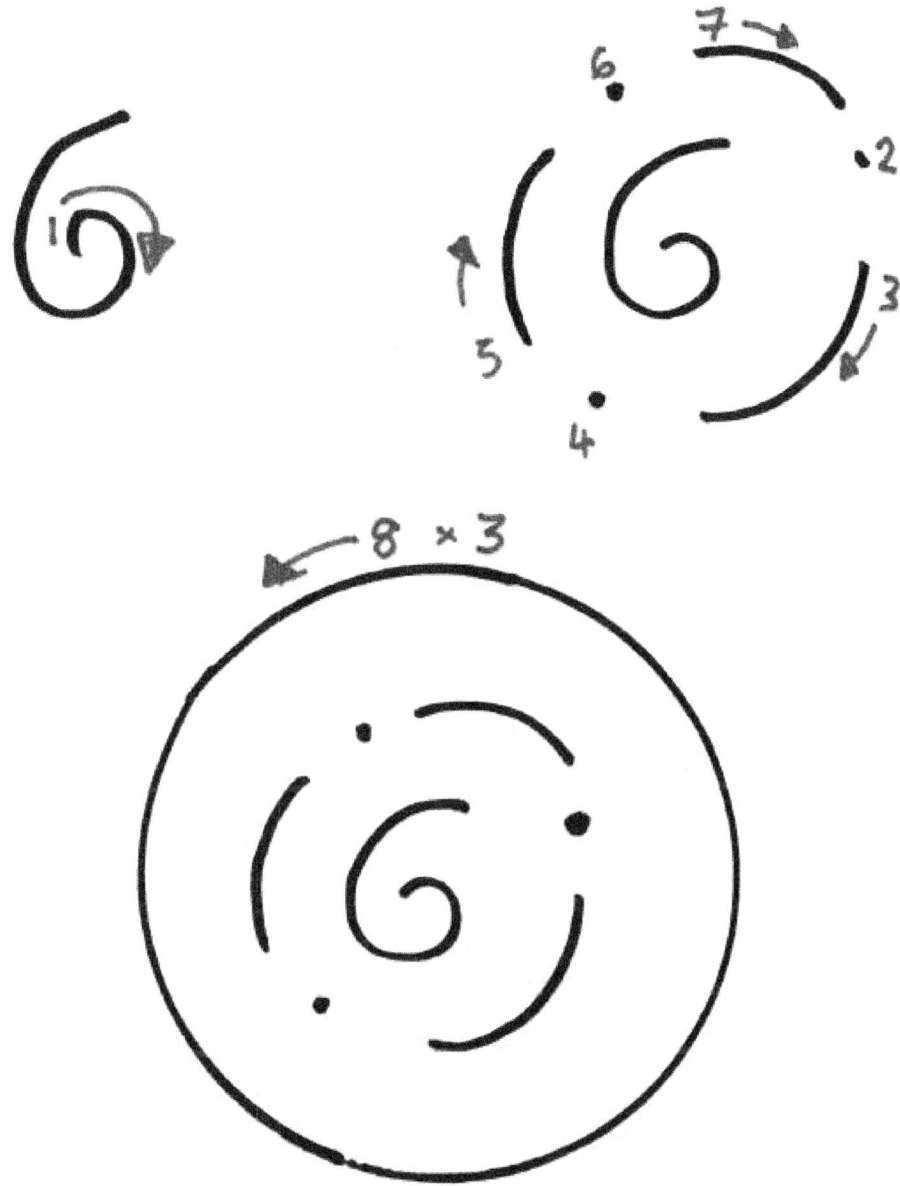

Elbow issues

Drawing instructions for a symbol to help with issues of the elbow:

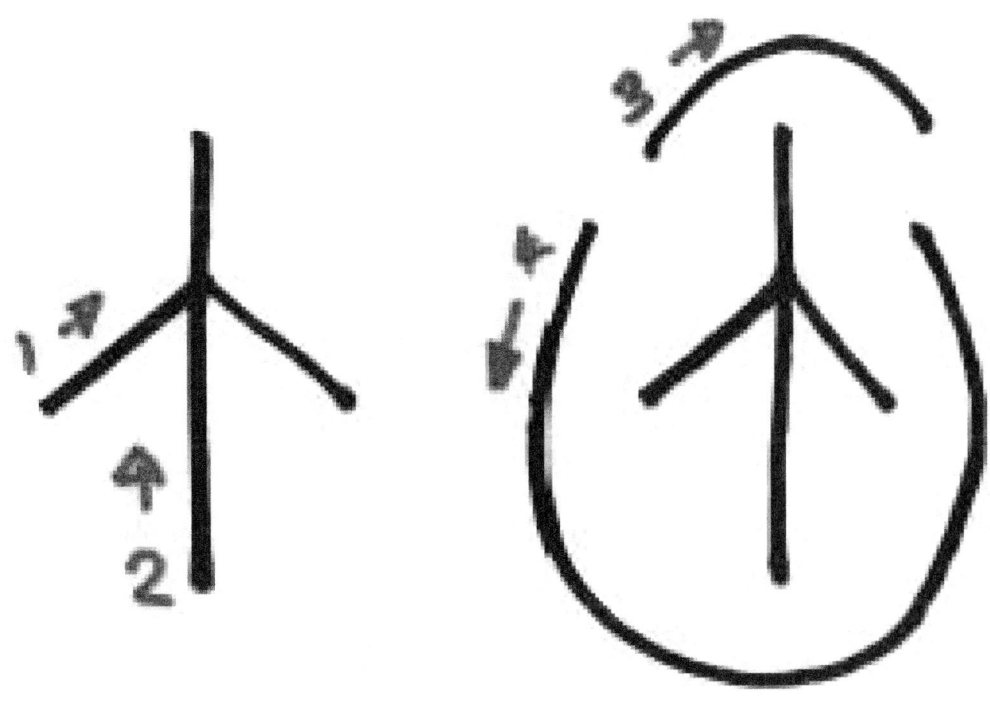

End of Life

Drawing instructions for a symbol to help with moving over to spirit peacefully:

Allowing the spirit to lift with ease. Line 1 is drawn or visualised beneath the animal. The rest of the symbol it is drawn vertically in the air.

Epilepsy

Epilepsy is a condition where sudden bursts of electrical activity in the brain cause seizures or fits. There are lots of possible symptoms of epilepsy seizures, including uncontrollable shaking.

Drawing instructions for a symbol to help with epilepsy:

Eyes

A symbol for overall eye health, from tired eyes, to severe issues.

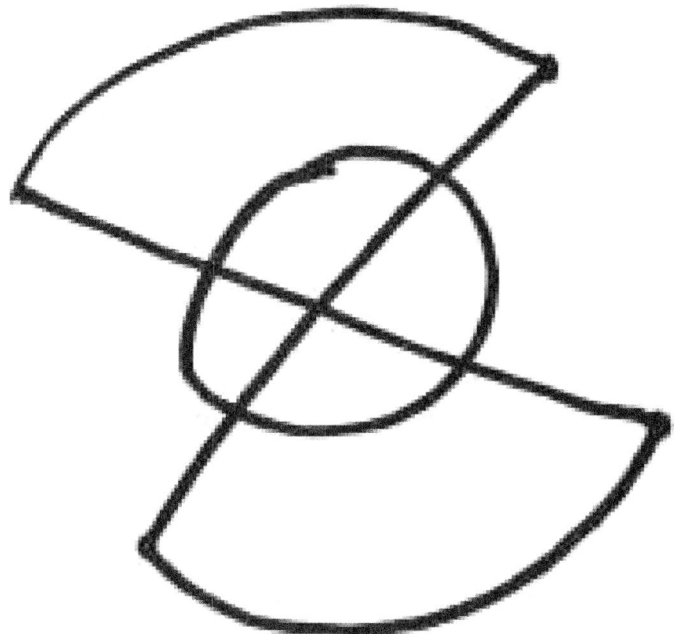

Drawing instructions for a symbol to help with eye issues

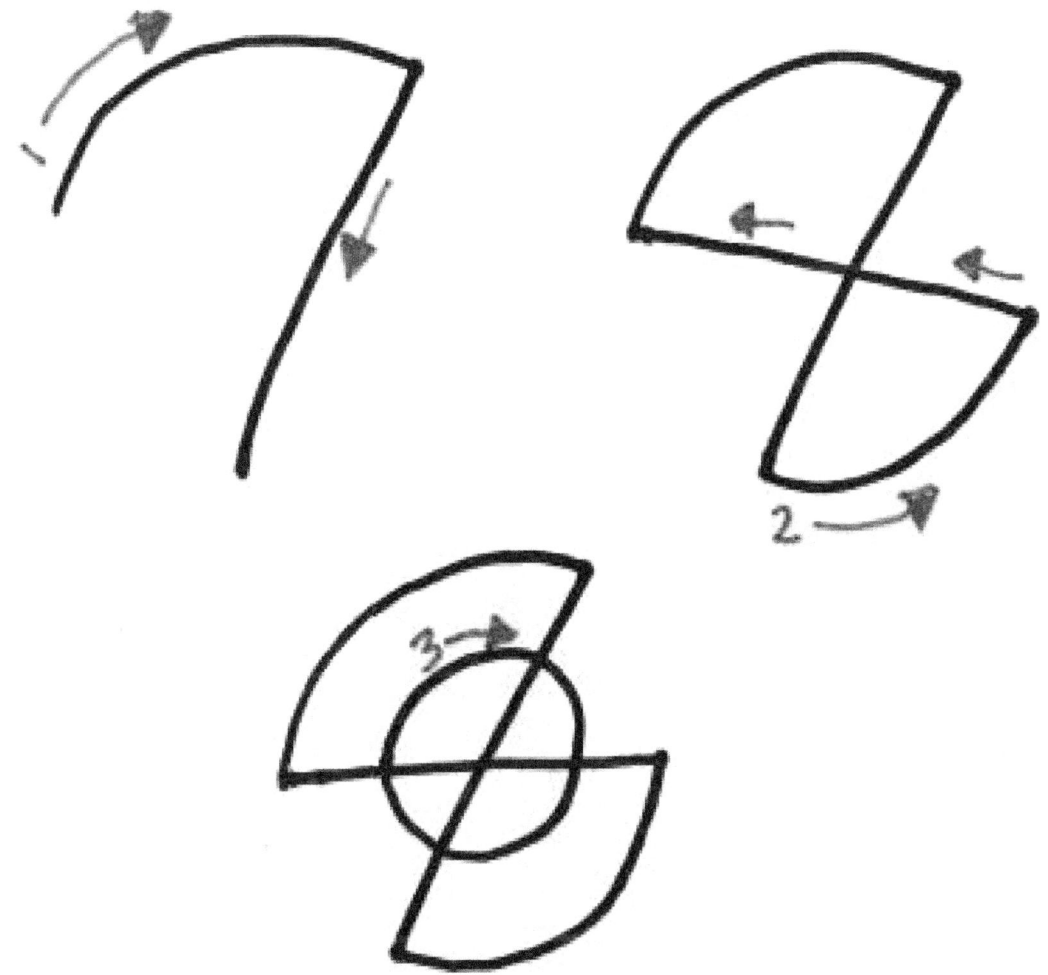

Feet issues

Drawing instructions for a symbol to help with foot issues:

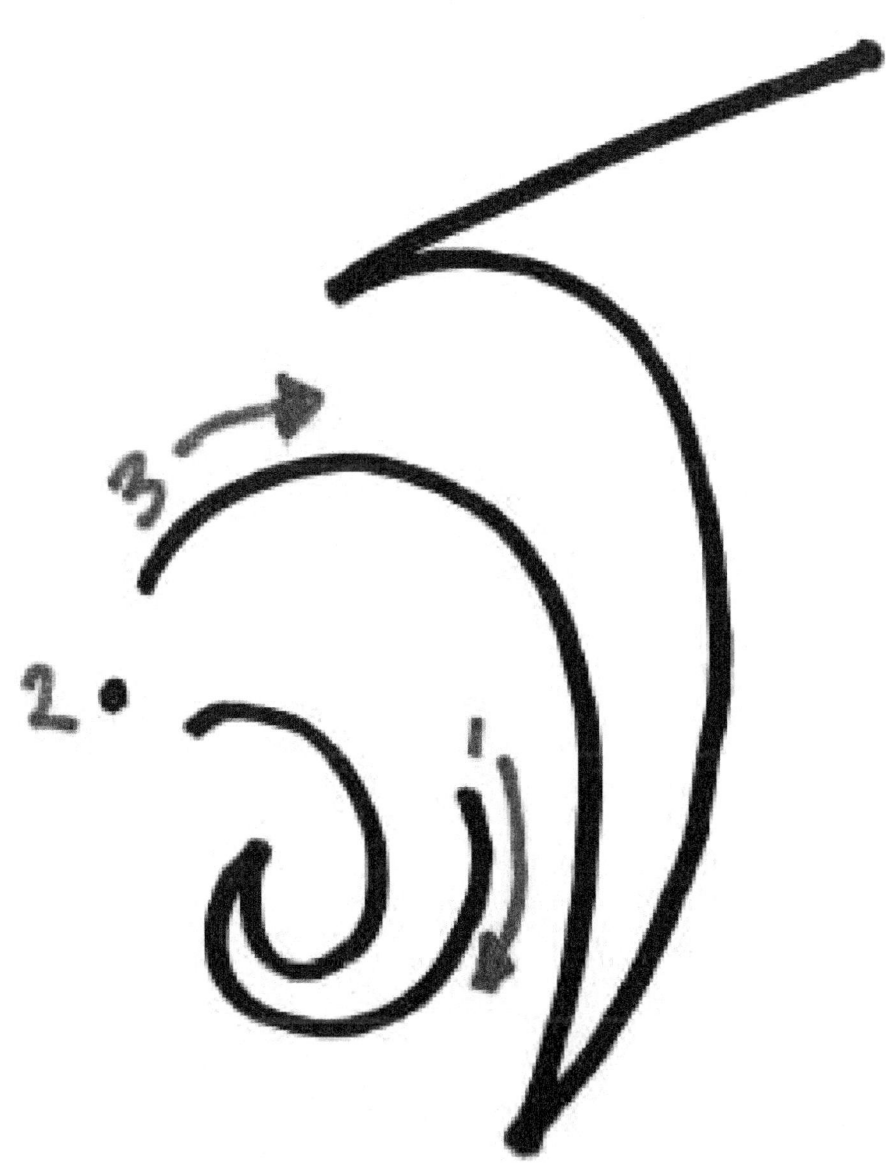

Flu

An infection of the nose, throat, and lungs. Symptoms include a high temperature, aching limbs, tiredness, and a headache.

Drawing instructions for a symbol to help with fly symptoms:

Flu (alternative)

Drawing instructions for Flu Symbol

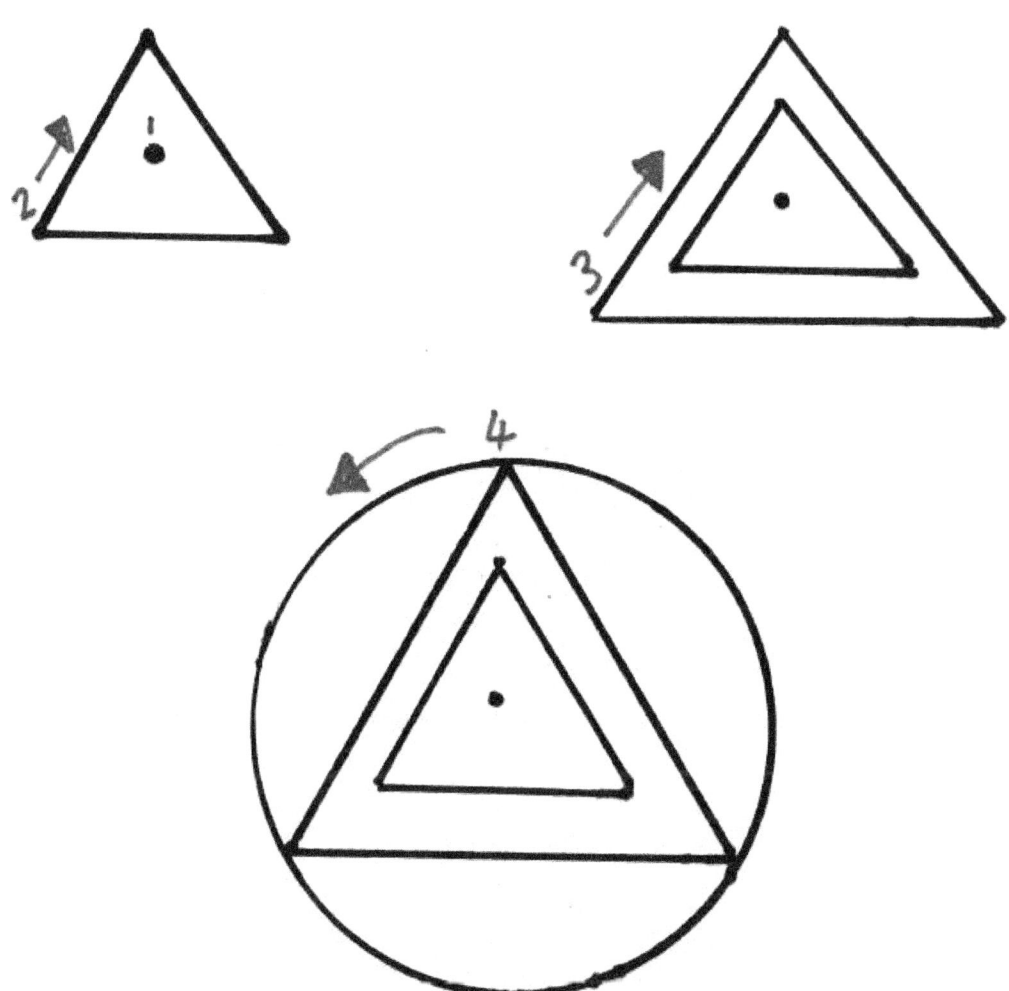

Guarding – items/ people/ places

Resource guarding is when a dog becomes defensive in order to keep you away from a particular item or "resource" that they treasure.

Drawing instructions for a symbol to help with resource guarding:

Visualise line number 2 going across the boundary that the animal is setting. The line disperses the energy of the boundary.

Hair loss

Hair loss (alopecia) can affect just patches or your entire body, and it can be temporary or permanent. It can be the result of heredity, hormonal changes or medical conditions.

Drawing instructions for a symbol to help with hair loss:

Head Issues

Drawing instructions for a symbol to help with issues of the head:

Line 1: trace around the aura of the head.

Line 2: draw from the centre of the head, down into the neck.

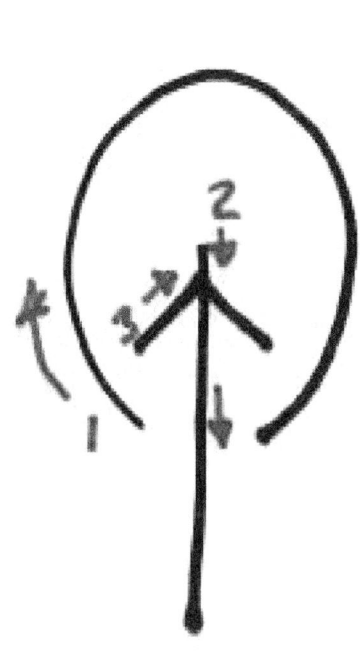
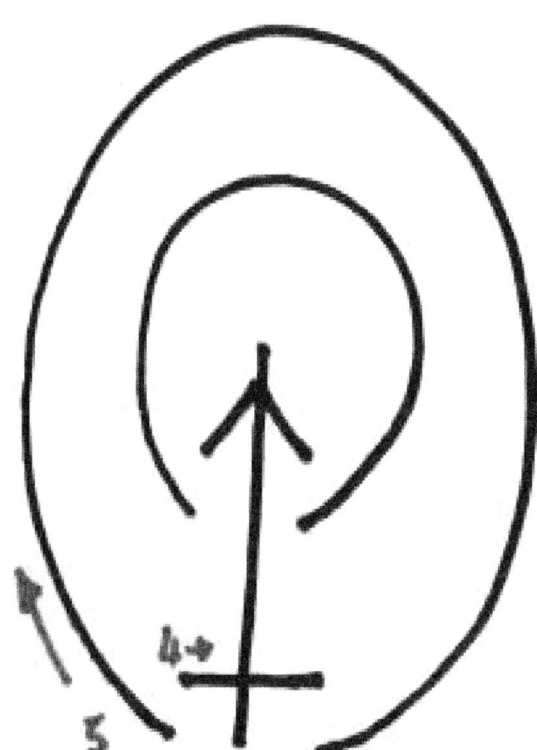

Headache

Headaches are classified as primary or secondary.

A primary headache means the headache itself is the main medical problem, although other factors, such as muscle tension or exposure to certain foods, may be identified. Other contributing factors include medicines, dehydration, or hormone changes.

A secondary headache is related to an underlying medical condition. An example of this would be a headache due to neck injury, eye problems, jaw, teeth or sinus infection.

Drawing instructions for a symbol to help with headache symptoms:

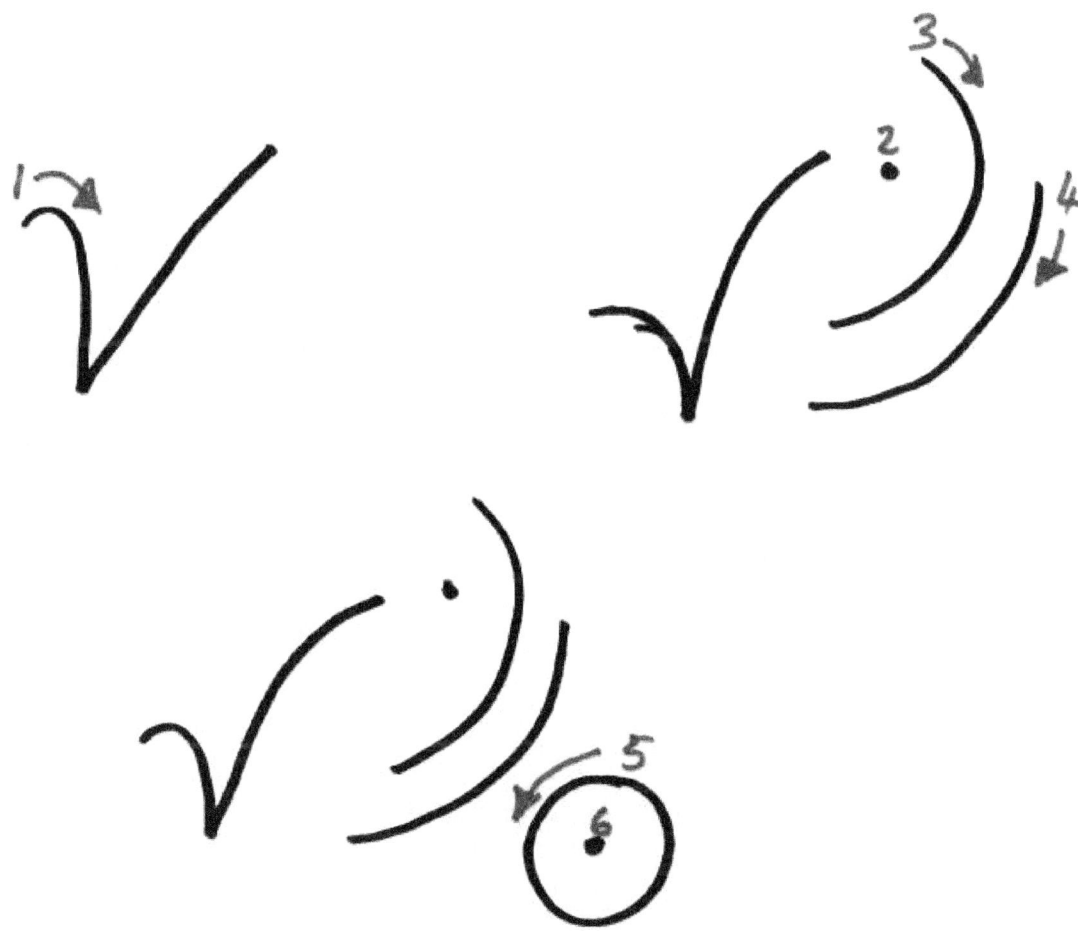

Headache (forehead)

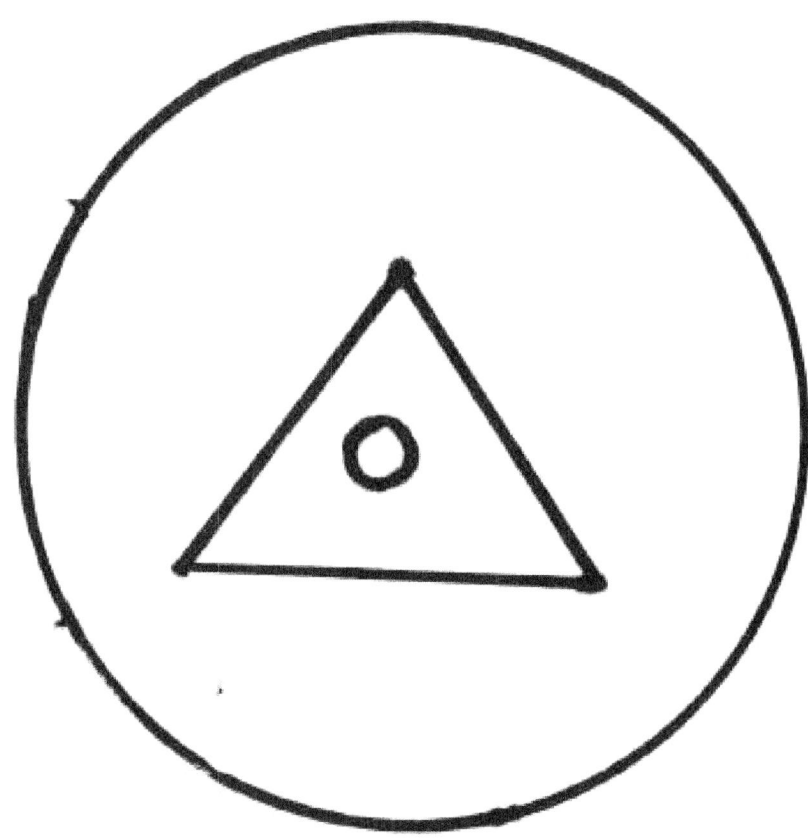

Drawing instructions

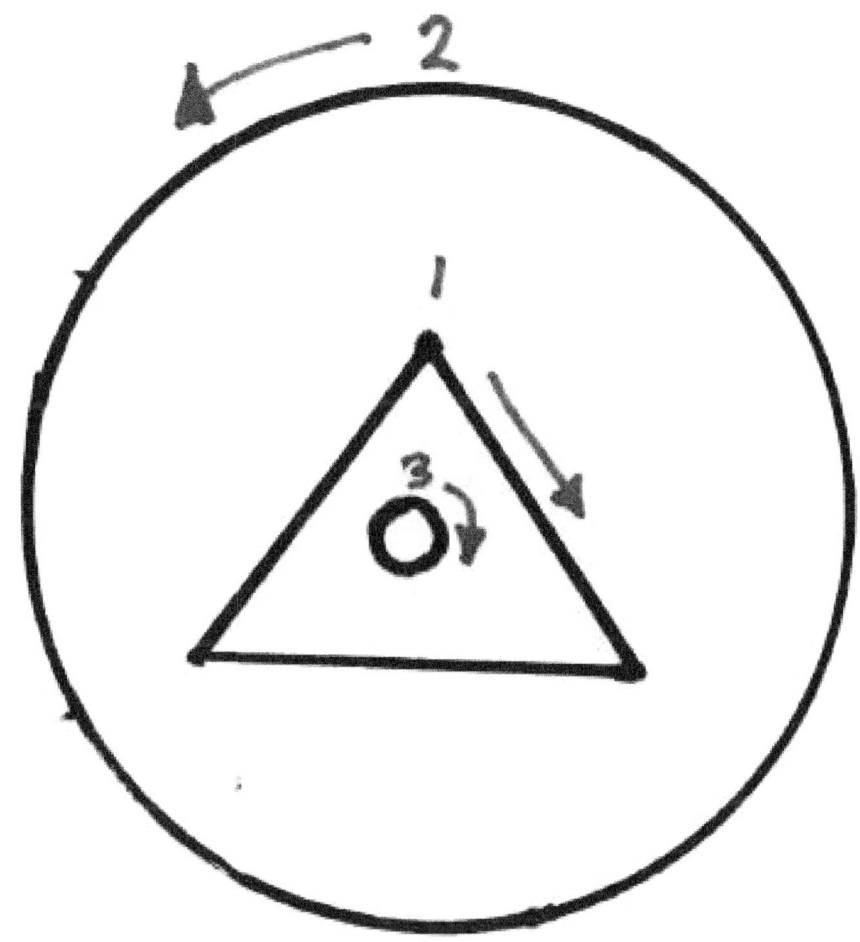

Heart Problems

When the heart isn't functioning well, it has trouble sending enough **blood**, oxygen and nutrients to the body. In a way, the heart delivers the fuel that keeps the body's systems running. If there's a problem with delivering that fuel, it affects everything the body's systems do.

Drawing instructions for a symbol to help with heart issues

Hip Issues

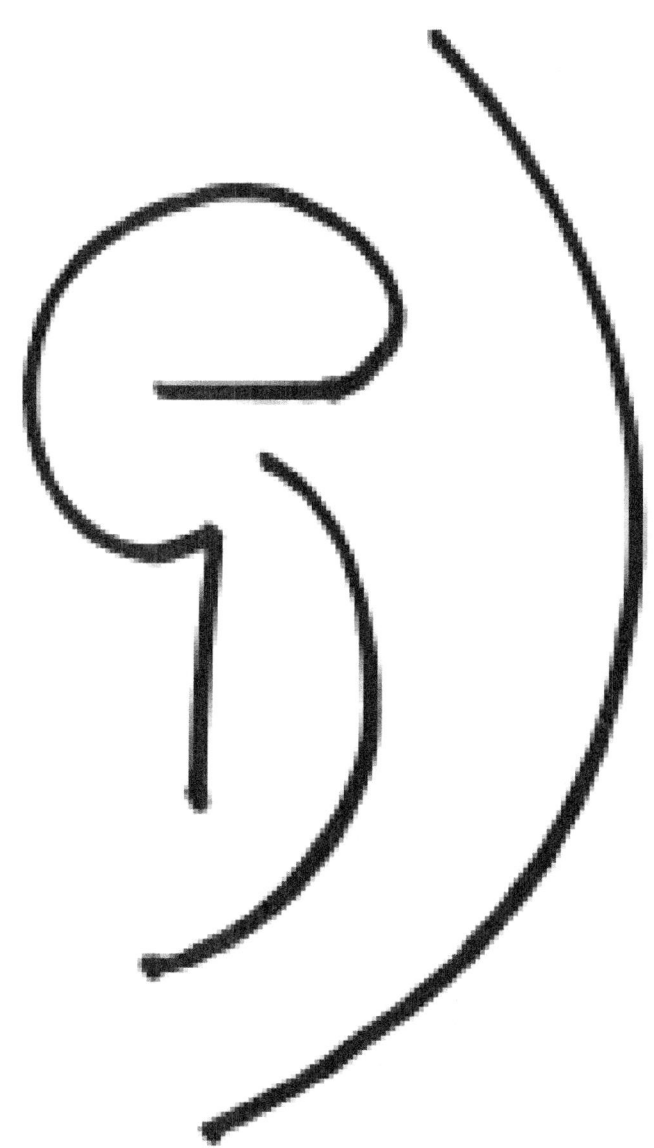

Drawing instructions for a symbol to help with issues of the hip:

Hock Issues

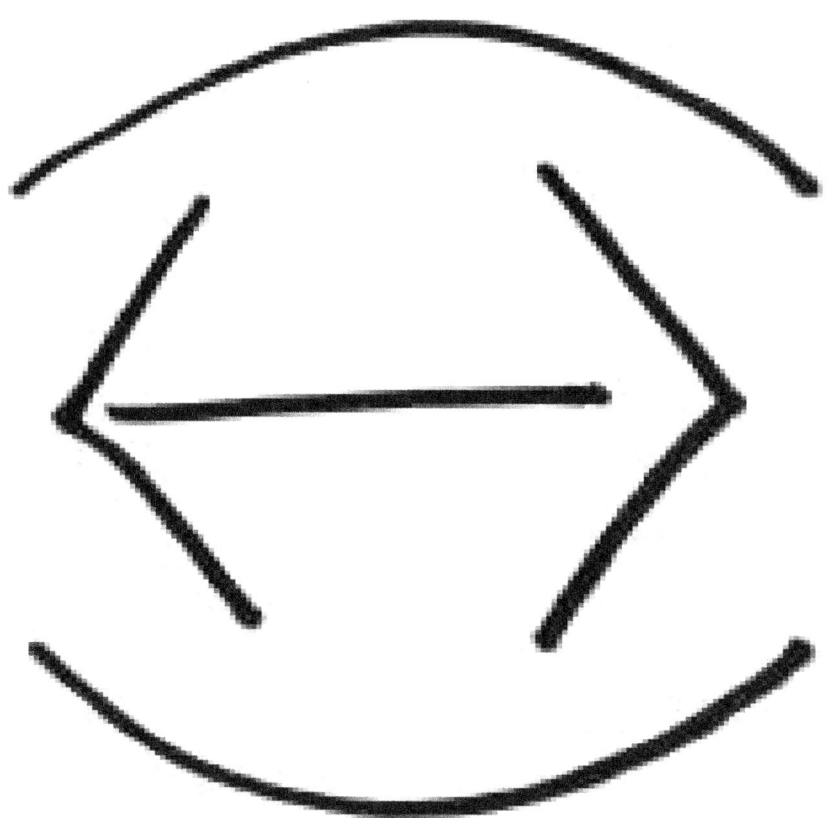

Drawing instructions for a symbol to help with hock issues:

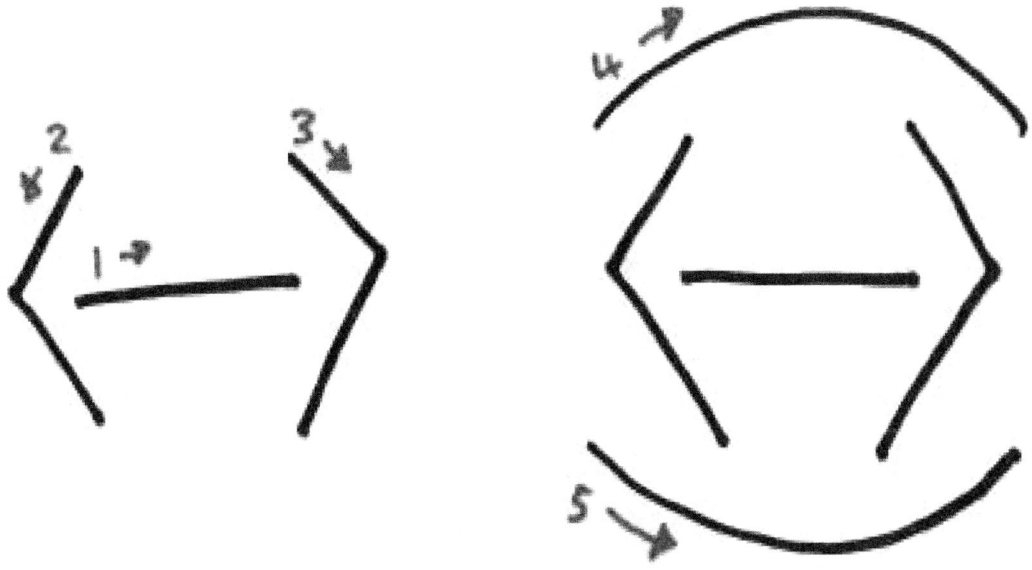

Hyperactive

Hyperactive behaviour generally refers to constant activity, being easily distracted, impulsiveness, inability to concentrate and can lead to aggressiveness. Typical behaviours may be fidgeting or constantly moving.

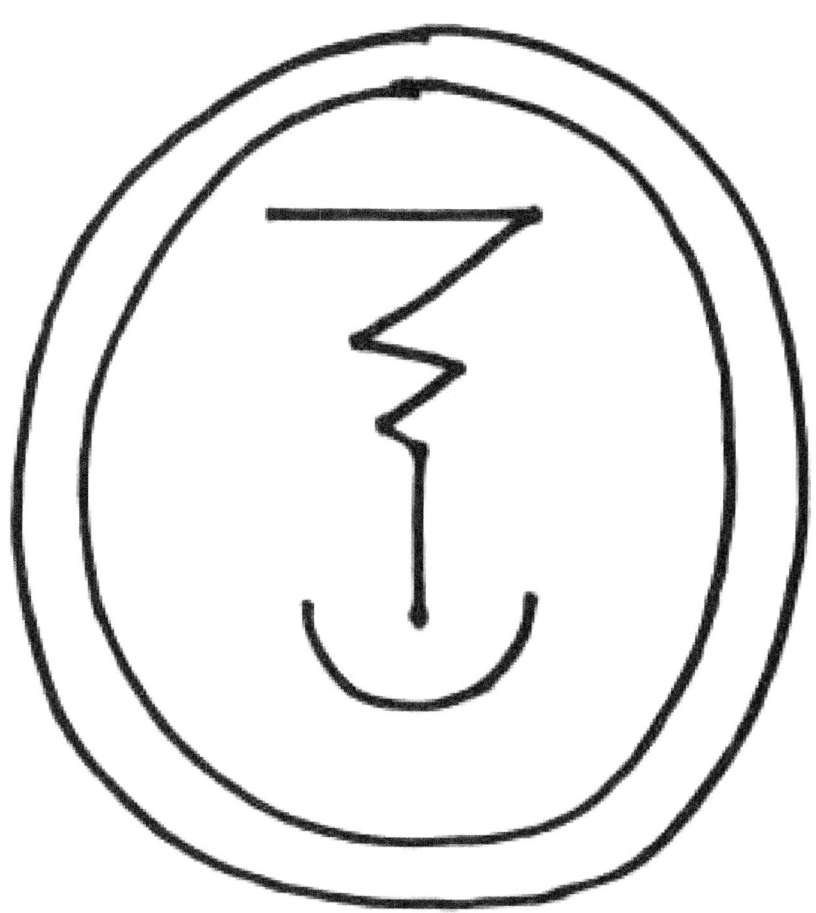

Drawing instructions for a symbol to help ease hyperactivity:

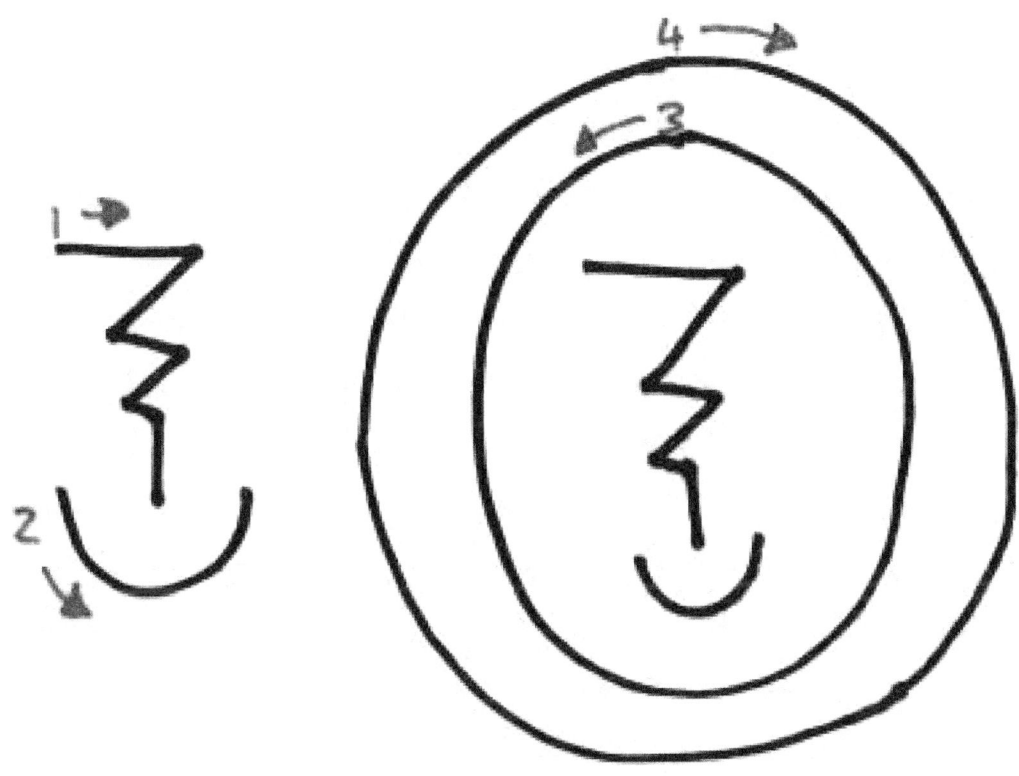

Infertility

The inability to conceive.

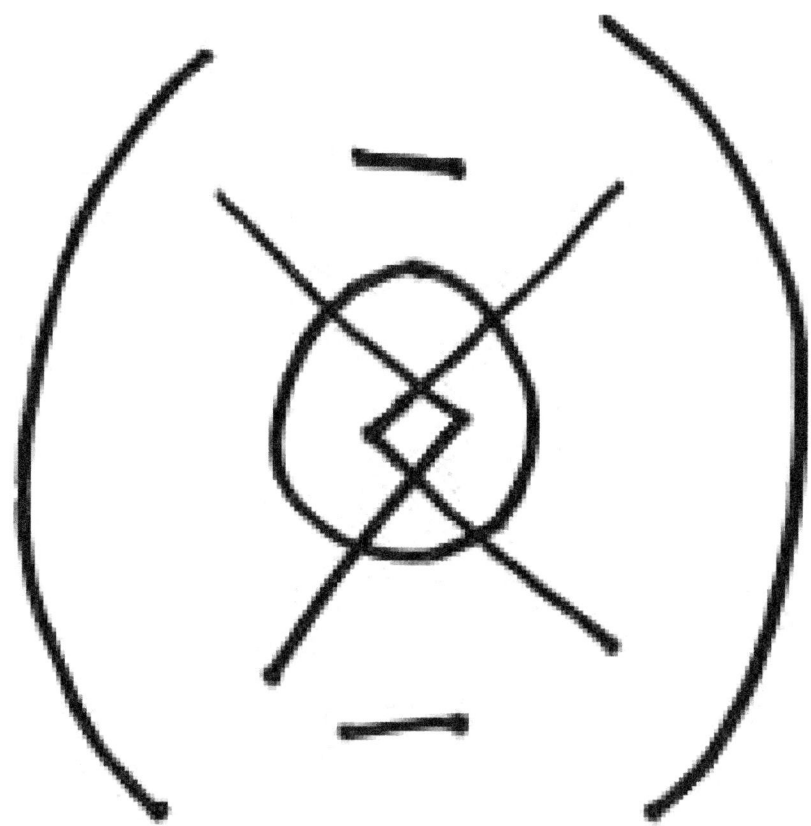

Drawing instructions for a symbol to help with infertility:

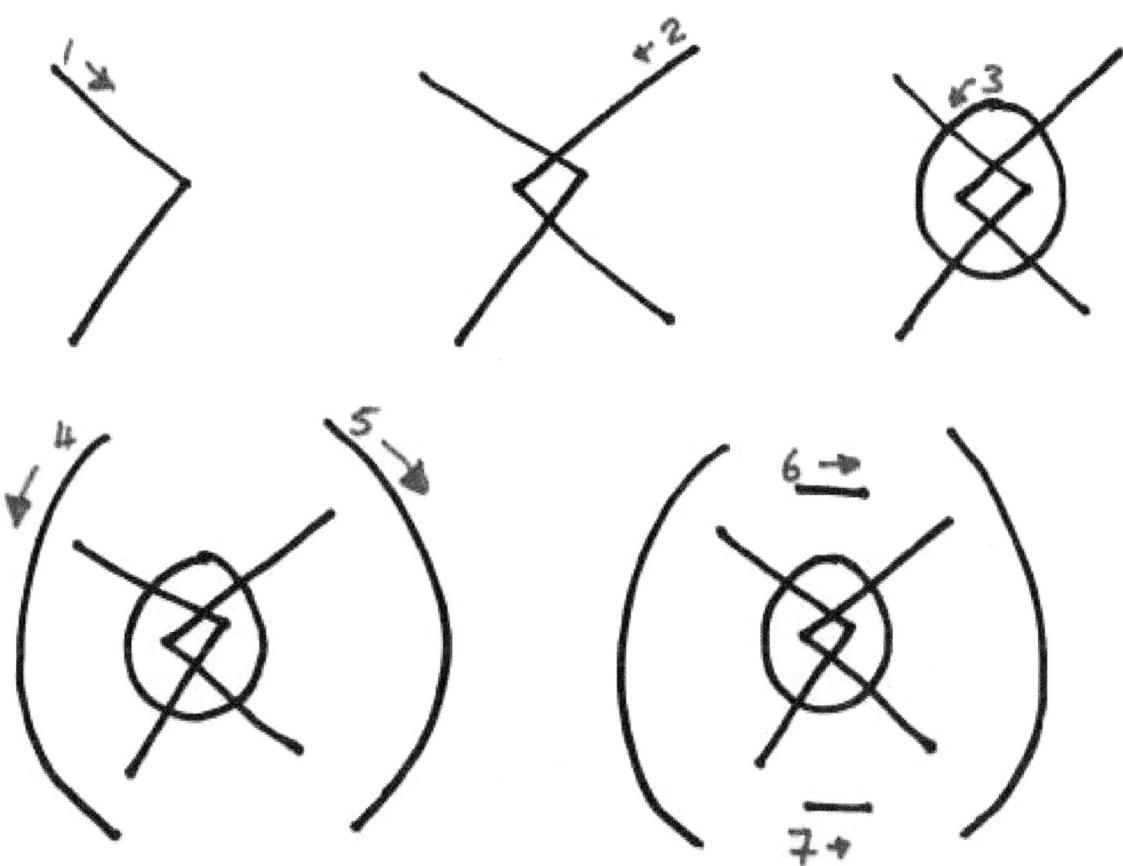

Insecurity / Fear

Uncertainty or anxiety including lack of confidence in oneself and others around them.

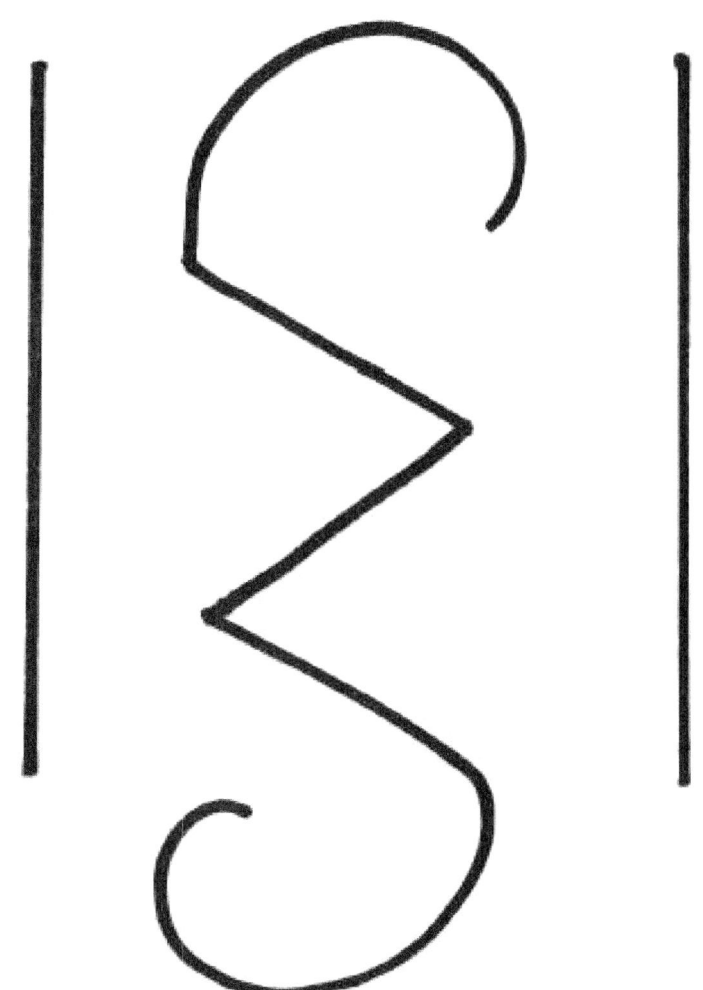

Drawing instructions for a symbol to promote feeling secure in one's surroundings.

This symbol helps with fear and anxiety due to an inner feeling of insecurity. Generally, it is drawn over the whole body.

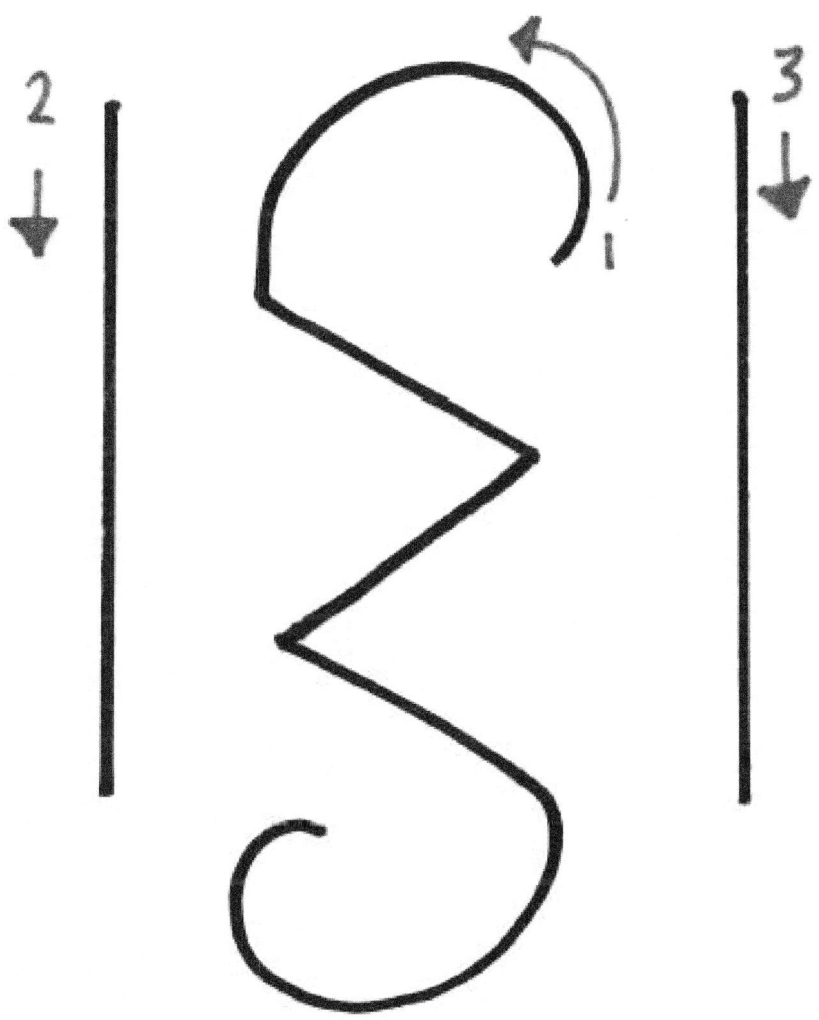

Joint Pain

Joint pain can be caused by many types of injuries or conditions. It may be linked to arthritis, bursitis, and muscle pain.

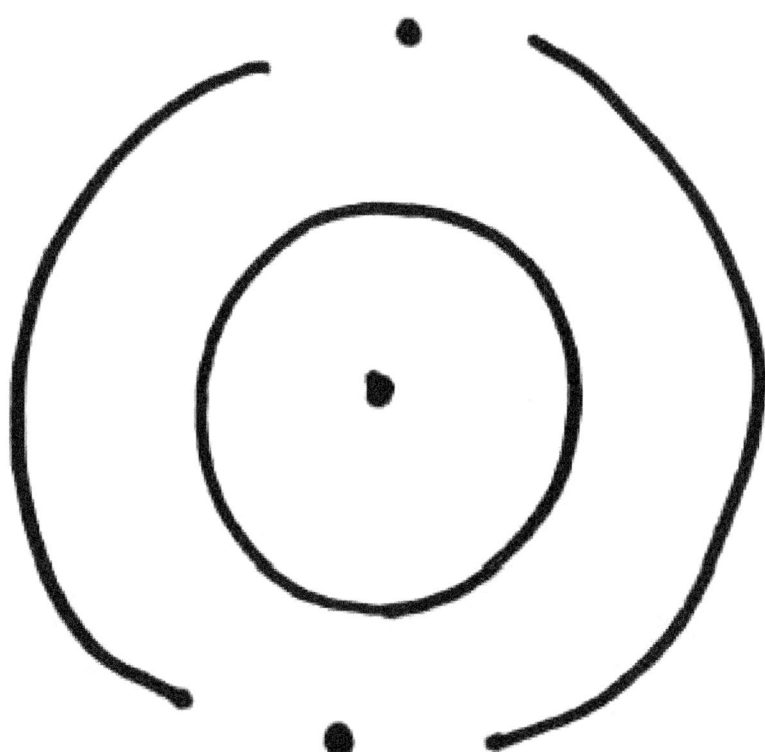

Drawing instructions for symbol to help with joint pain:

The first circle should be drawn around the painful area.

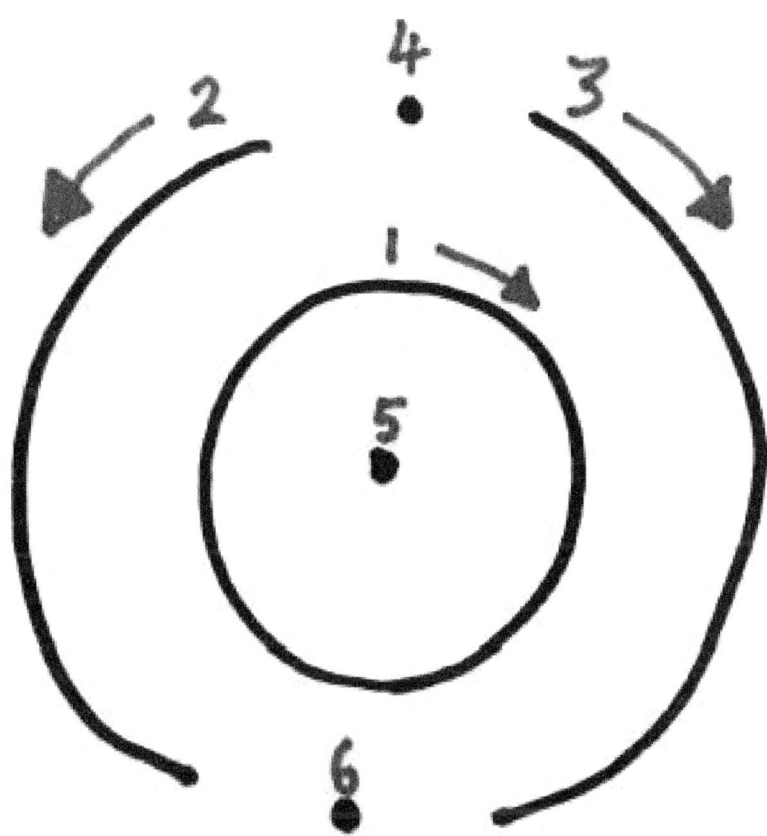

Kidneys

Kidneys are a special filter system for the body. The kidneys remove waste products from the blood and produce urine. They control the levels of many substances in the blood and help to control your blood pressure.

Drawing instructions for a symbol to help with kidney issues:

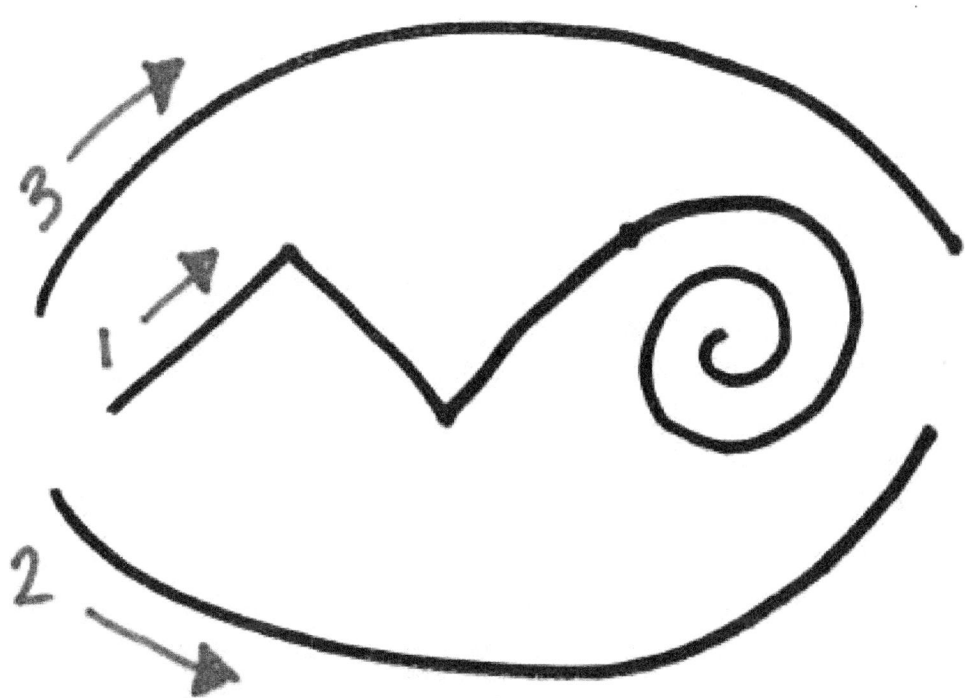

Knee Issues

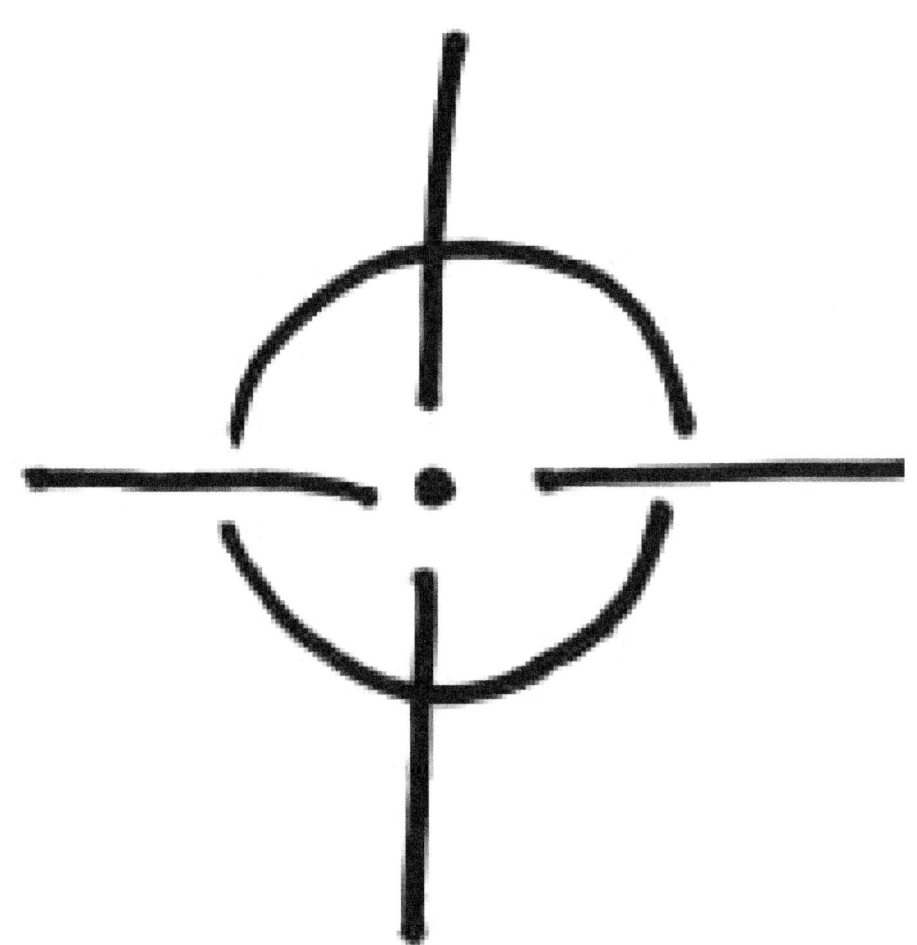

Drawing instructions for a symbol to help with issues of the knee:

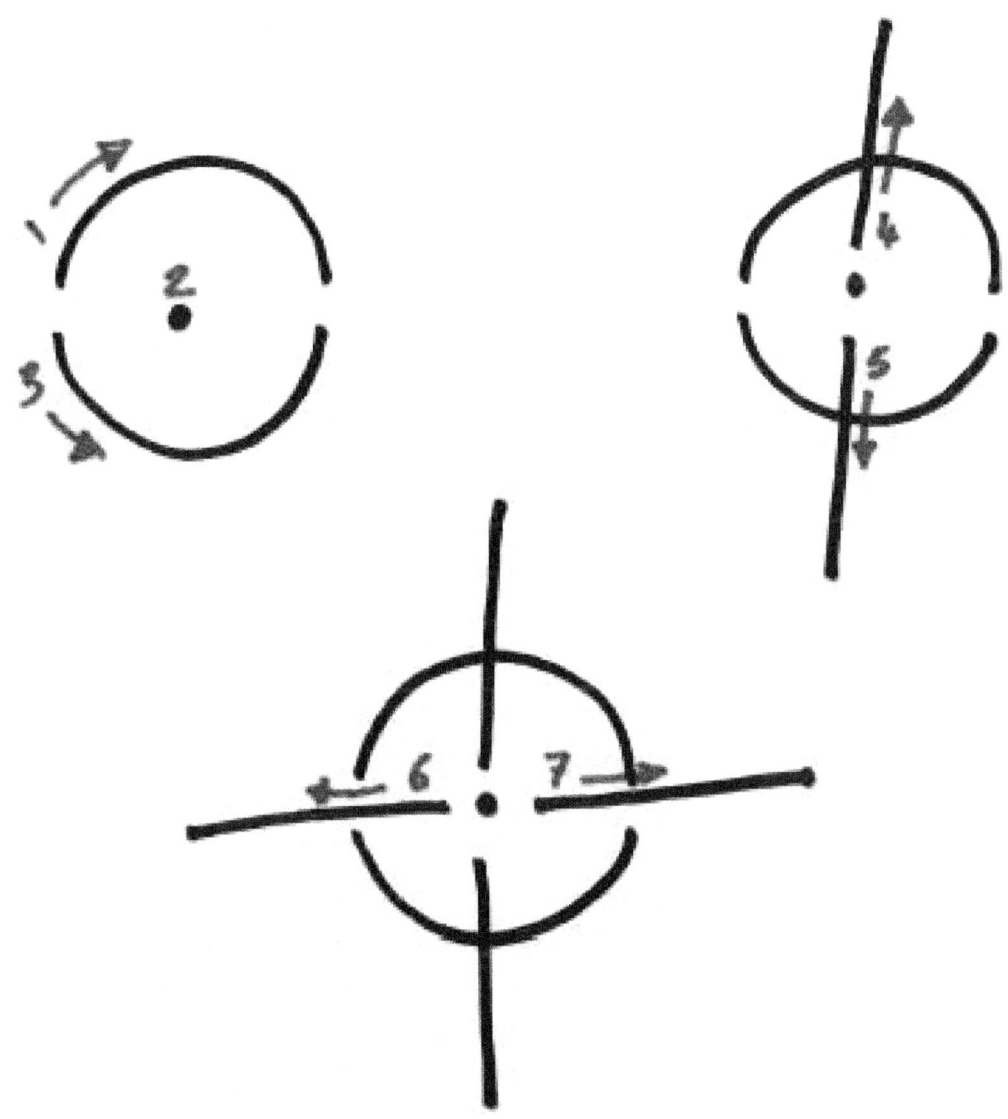

Laminitis

Laminitis is inflammation and damage of the tissue between the hoof and the underlying coffin bone. In severe cases, the hoof and coffin bone are separated and the coffin bone can rotate, leading to severe pain. It is a common, extremely painful and frequently recurrent condition in horses, ponies and donkeys.

Drawing instructions for a symbol to help with the symptoms of laminitis and those horses prone to it

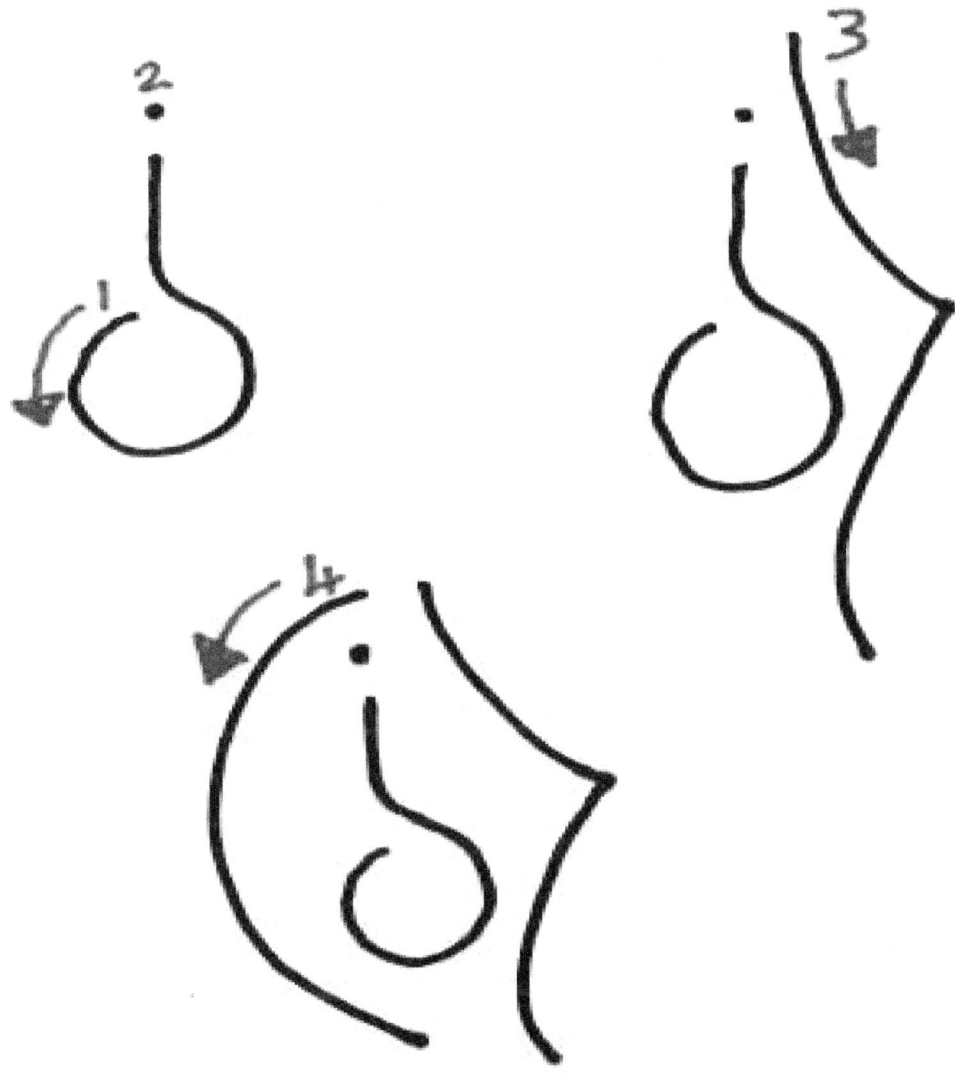

Leg Issues

Drawing instructions for a symbol to help with issues of the legs:

Lethargy

A lack of energy and enthusiasm.

Drawing instructions for a symbol to help with lethargic animals:

Licking (excessive)

Excessive licking is a compulsive behaviour which can affect any dog, of either gender, of any age and of any breed.

Drawing instructions for a symbol to help with excessive licking:

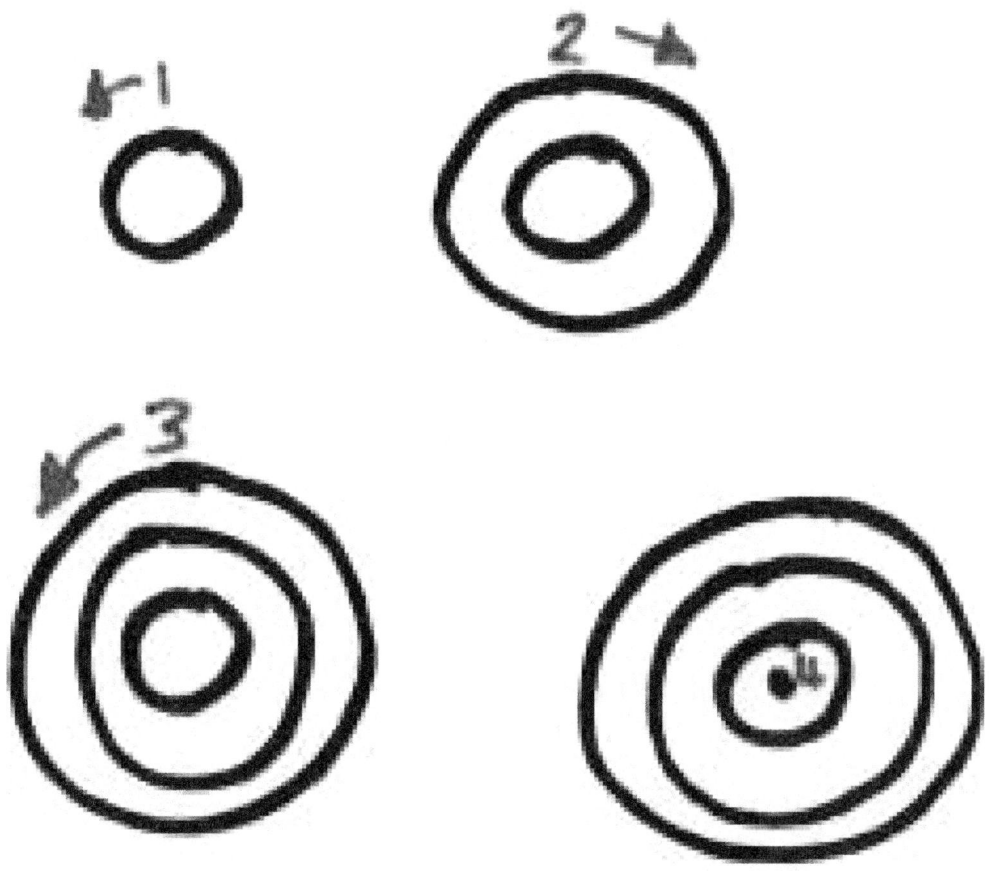

Liver

The liver regulates most chemical levels in the blood. It excretes a product called bile. This helps to carry away waste products from the liver. All the blood leaving the stomach and intestines passes through the liver. The liver processes this blood and breaks down, balances, and creates the nutrients. More than 500 vital functions have been identified with the liver.

Drawing instructions for a symbol to help with liver problems:

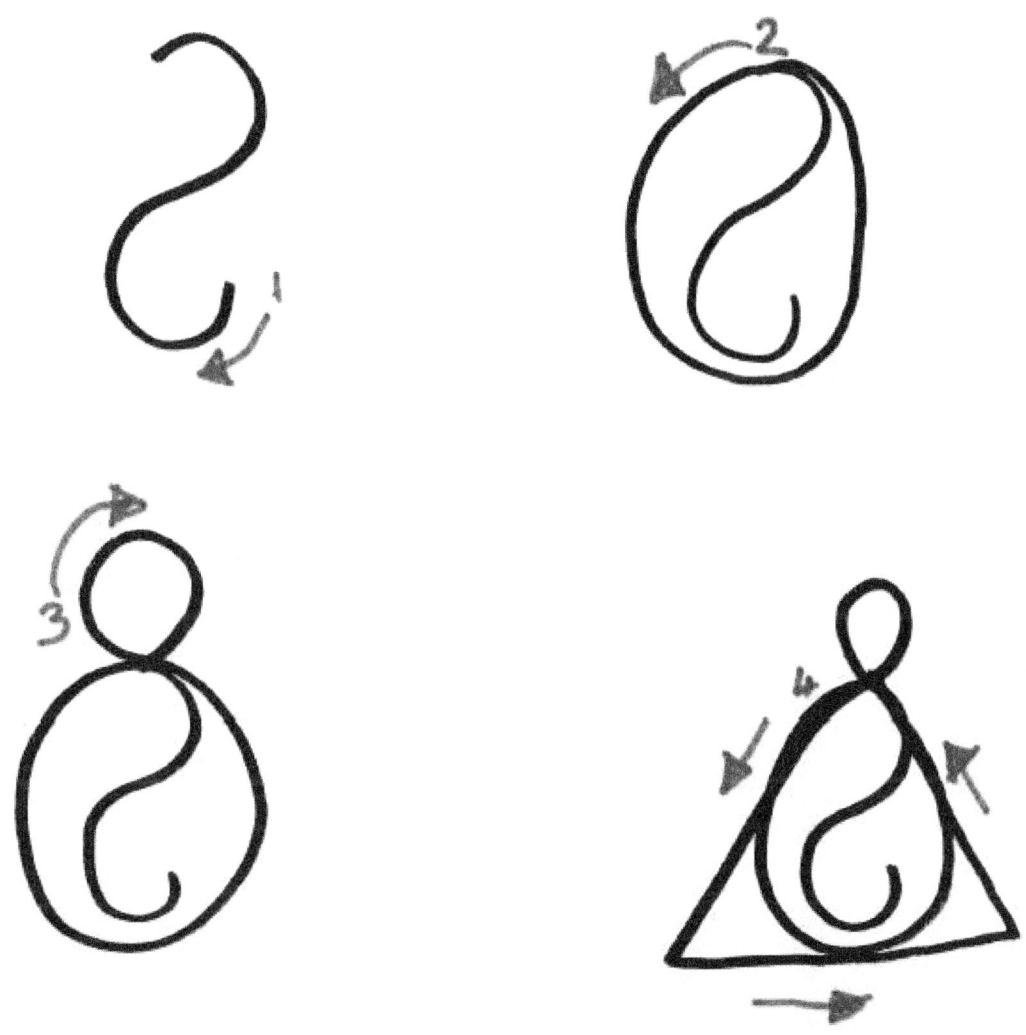

Loss

This symbol helps with the feelings of loss when a loved one has passed or is no longer with us, for whatever the reason

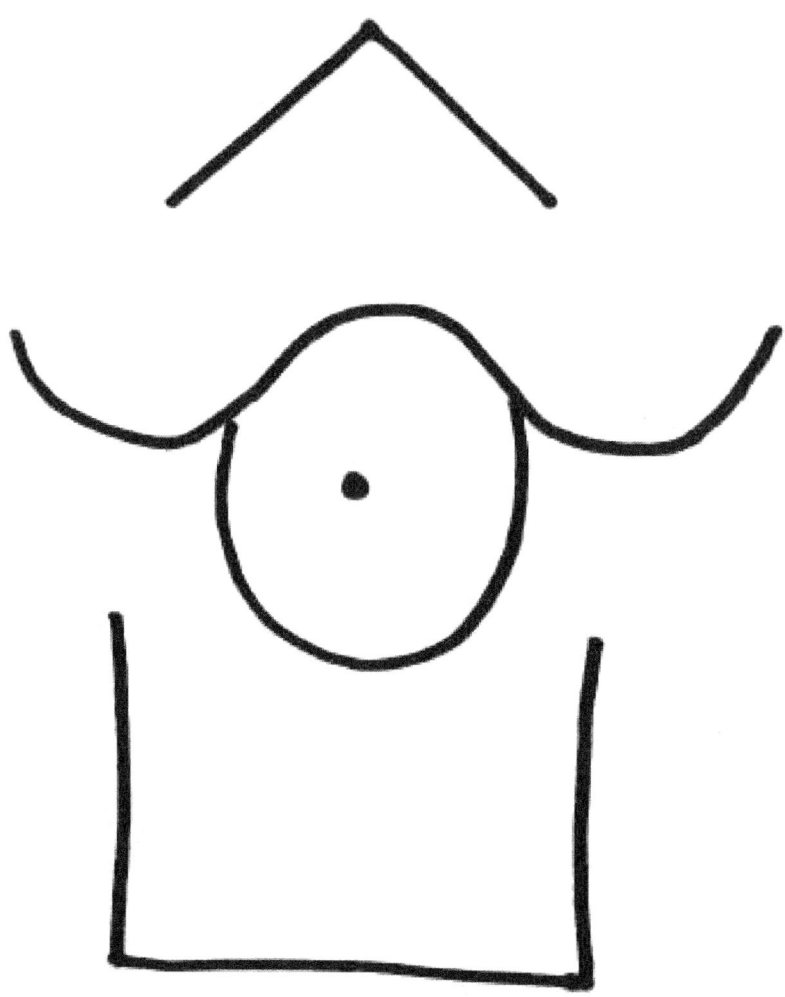

Drawing instructions for a symbol to help with loss:

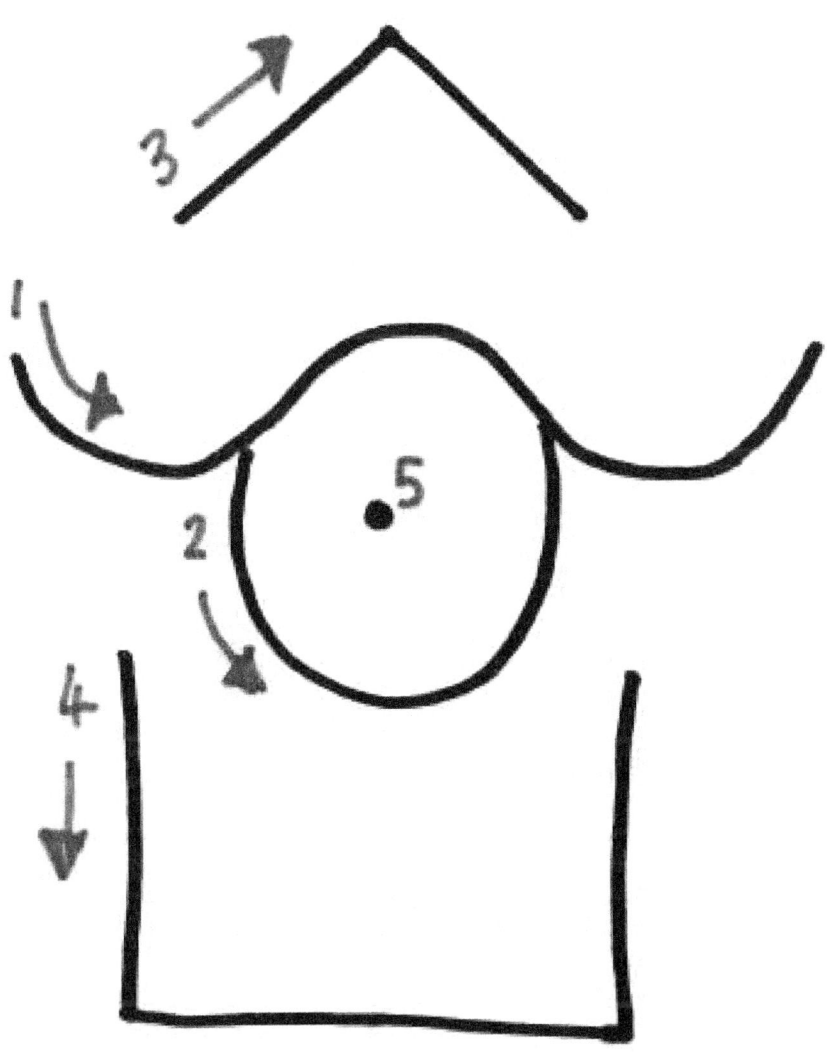

Lungs

Lungs are part of the body's **respiratory system**. All animals that have a backbone and breathe **air** have lungs. When an animal inhales, air filled with oxygen flows into the lungs. When an animal exhales, carbon dioxide and water vapor flow out of the lungs.

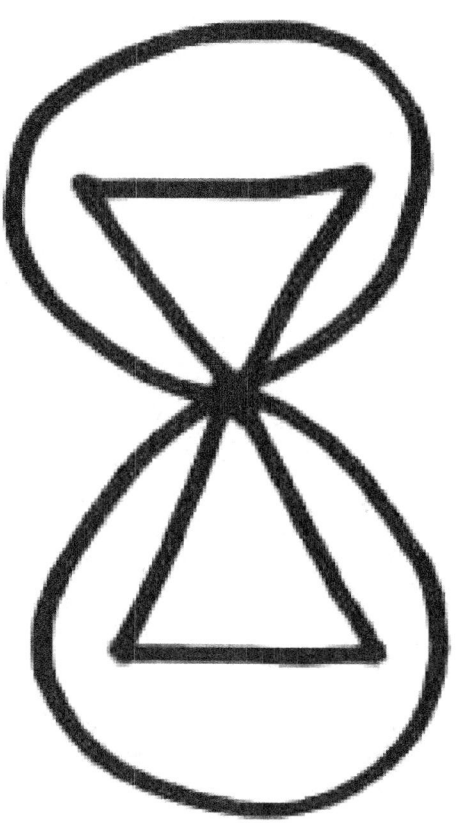

Drawing instructions for a symbol to help with lung issues:

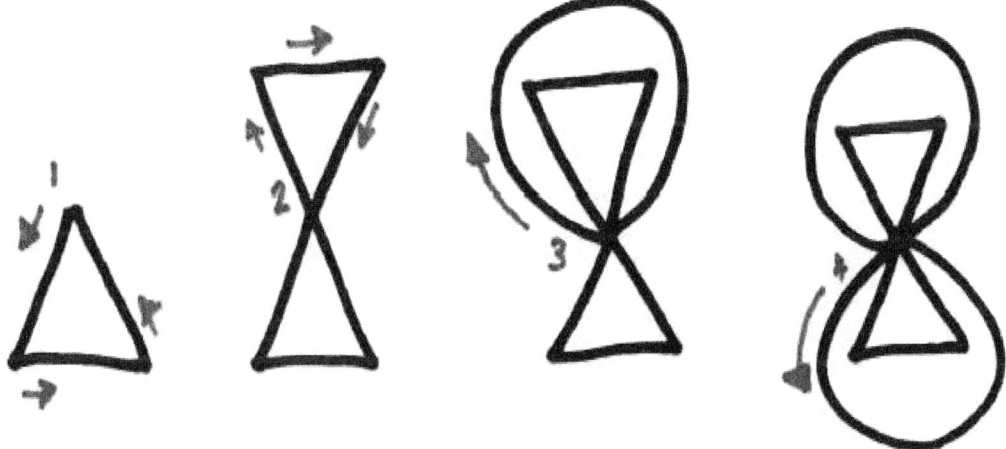

Mouth issues

Drawing instructions for a symbol to help with any issue in the mouth:

Navicular

Navicular syndrome describes a condition where pain arises from the navicular bone in the foot and the surrounding soft tissue structures.

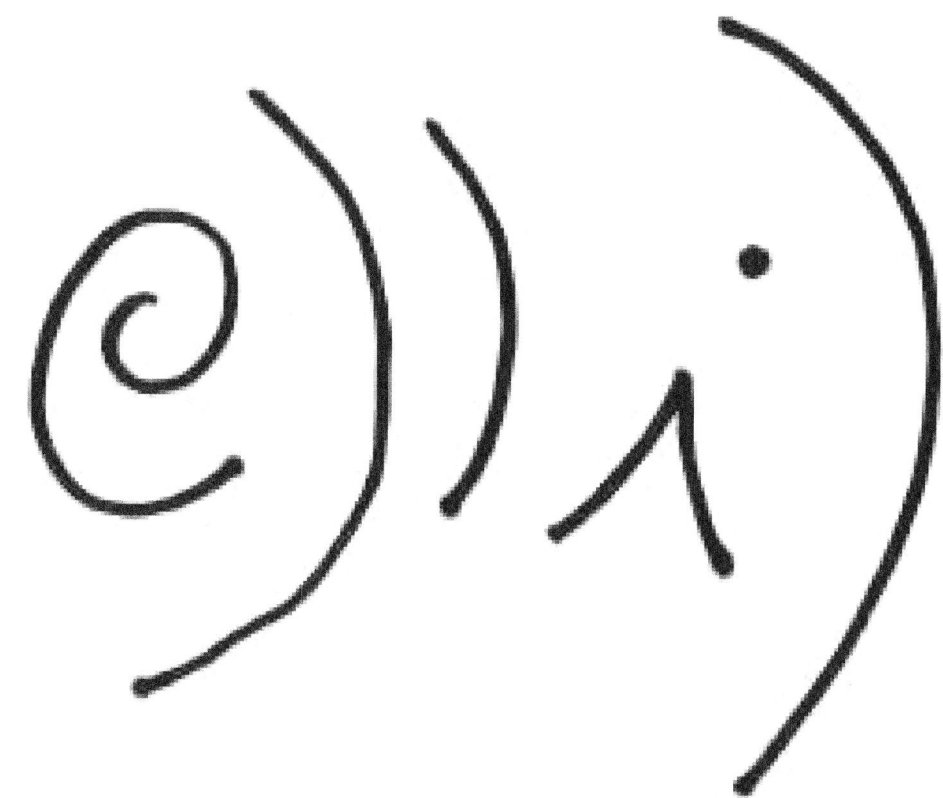

Drawing instructions for a symbol to help with the symptoms of navicular:

Neck Issues

Drawing instructions for a symbol to help with neck issues:

Nervous Aggression

Nervous or fear aggression happens when an animal wants to increase distance between himself and a trigger (commonly another animal or a human).

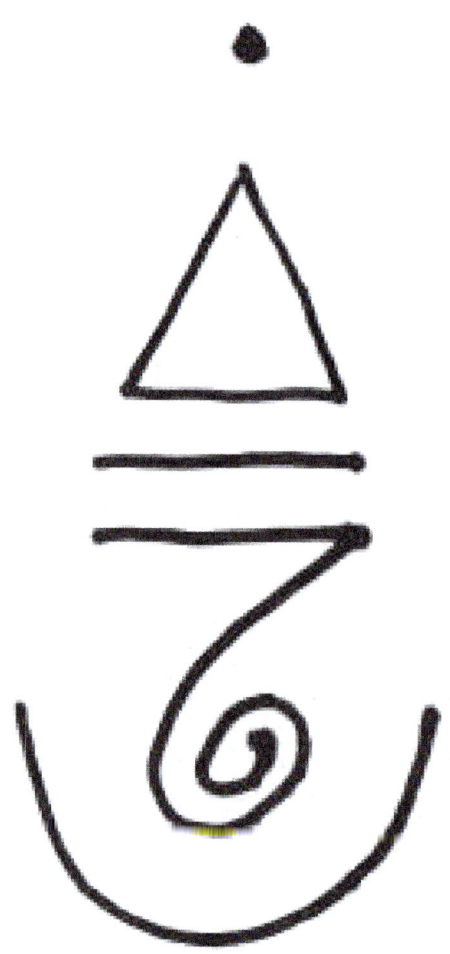

Drawing instructions for a symbol to help with nervous aggression:

Noise Reactive

Noise aversion or noise anxiety occurs when an animal reacts to loud noises.

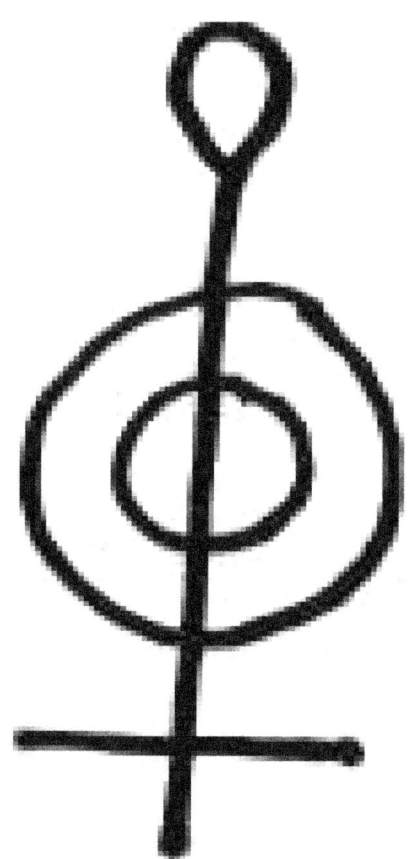

Drawing instructions for a symbol to help animals that are caused stress by loud noises:

Nose Issues

Drawing instructions for a symbol to help with issues of the nose:

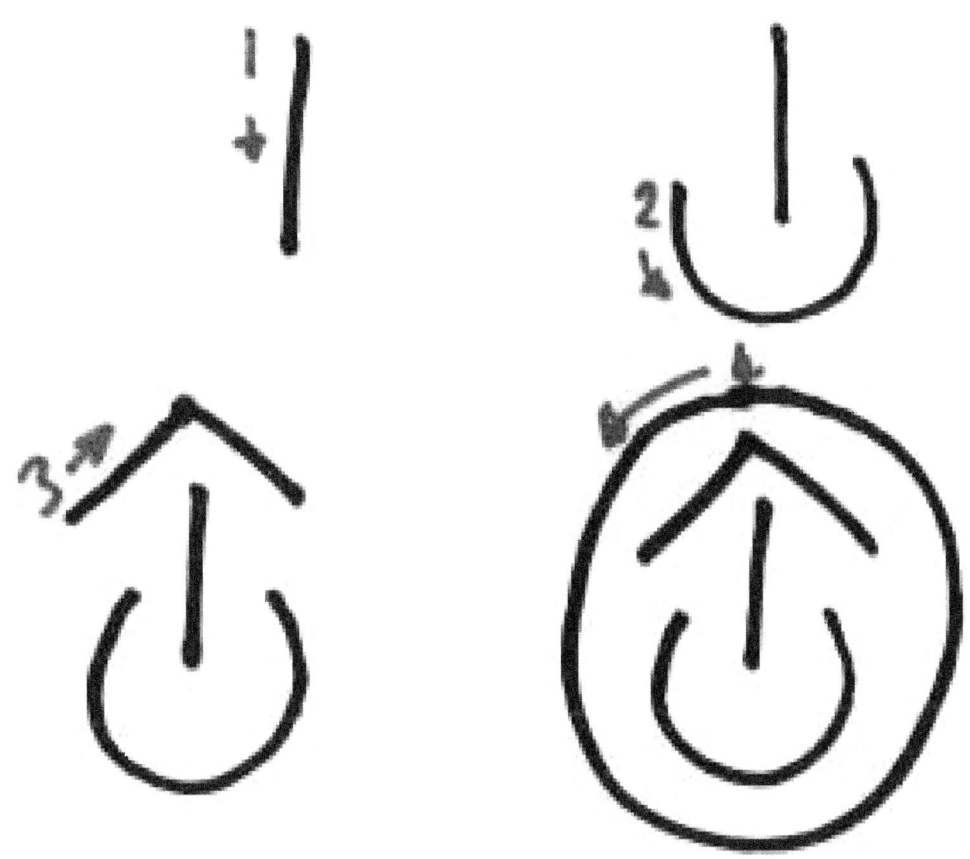

Overprotective

Excessive protectiveness can be a dangerous situation. Some dogs resort to aggressive behaviours to prevent strangers or even family members from getting too close to their owners.

Drawing instructions for a symbol to help with over protective animals:

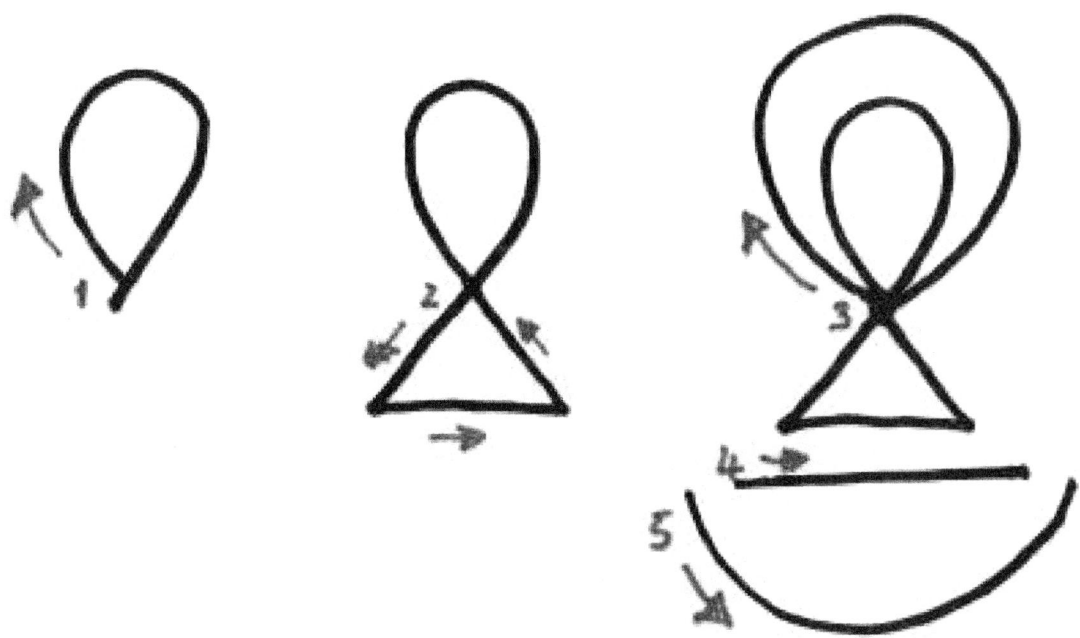

Owner Stress

This symbol works with a variety of stressors for the owner. From helping the owner before competition to helping the owner when they are worried about their animal. Whether they be ill or for any other reason.

It is also useful when working with your own animals, where you will no doubt be emotionally involved in the situation and outcome. This can make it harder to connect to the animal.

Drawing instructions for a symbol to help with owner stress that may be affecting the animal:

Often drawn over the heart or solar plexus of the owner – wherever you can feel the tension in your body.

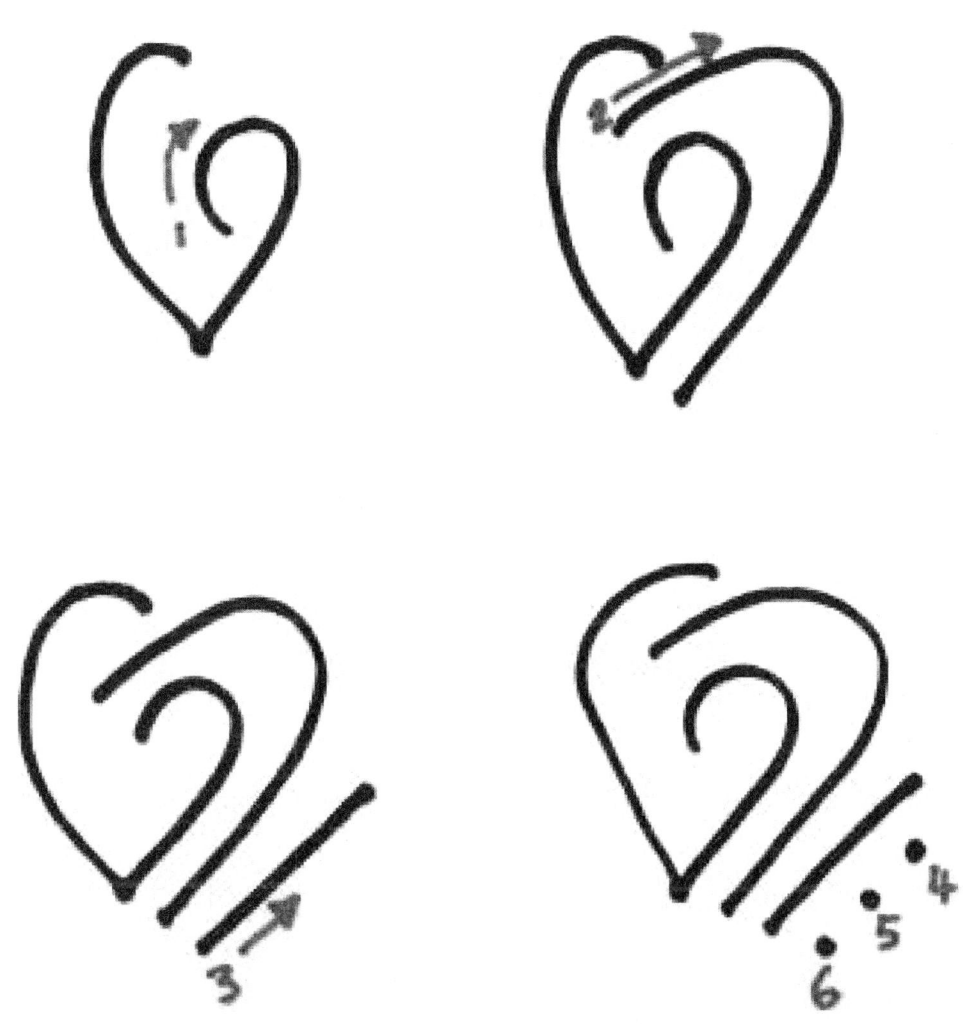

Drawing instructions for a symbol to help with issues of the pastern:

Pelvis Issues

Drawing instructions for a symbol to help with pelvis issues:

Poisoning

Poisons can be swallowed, inhaled, absorbed through the skin, injected or splashed into the eyes. Immediate veterinary attention is advised.

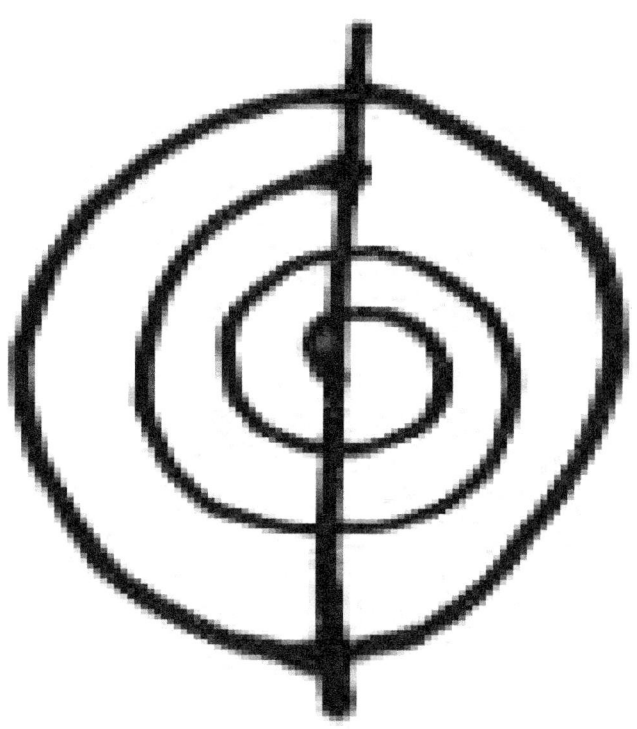

Drawing instructions for a symbol to help with the symptoms of poisoning

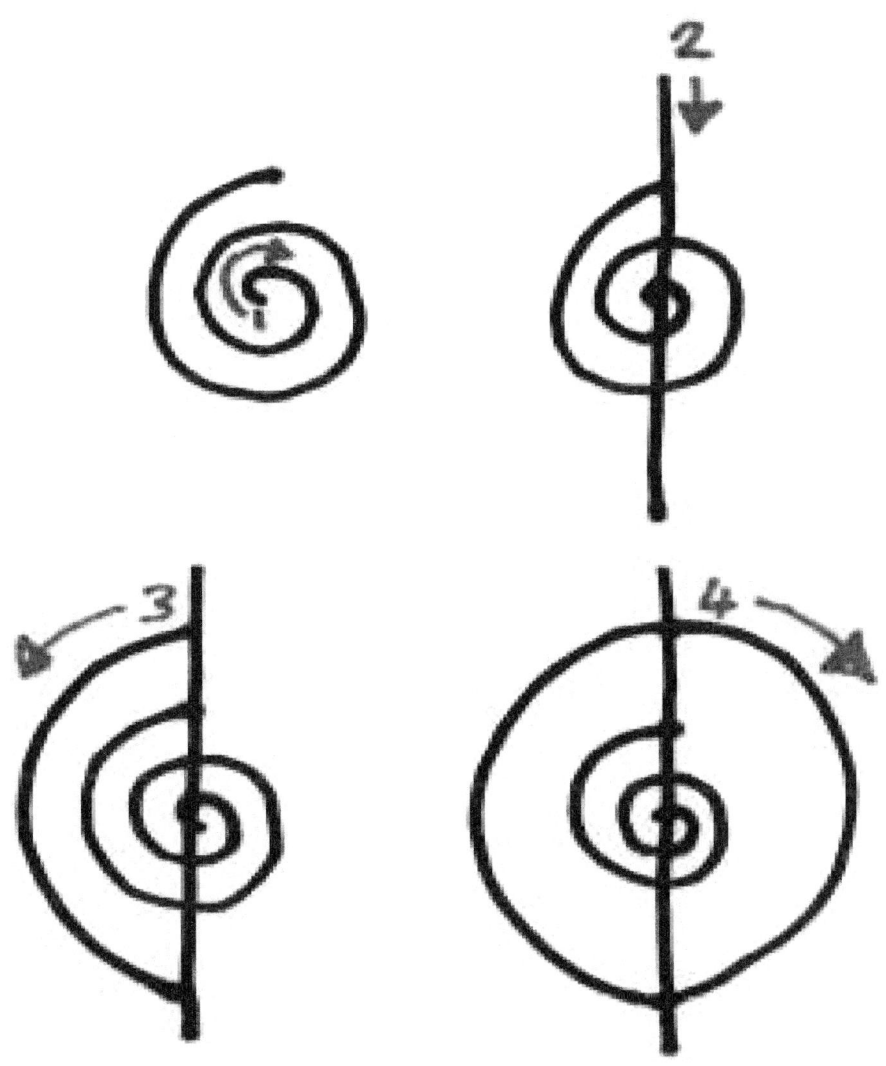

Reproductive Cycle Issues

The menstrual cycle is complex. It is controlled by many different glands and the hormones that these glands produce.

Drawing instructions for a symbol to help with reproductive cycle issues

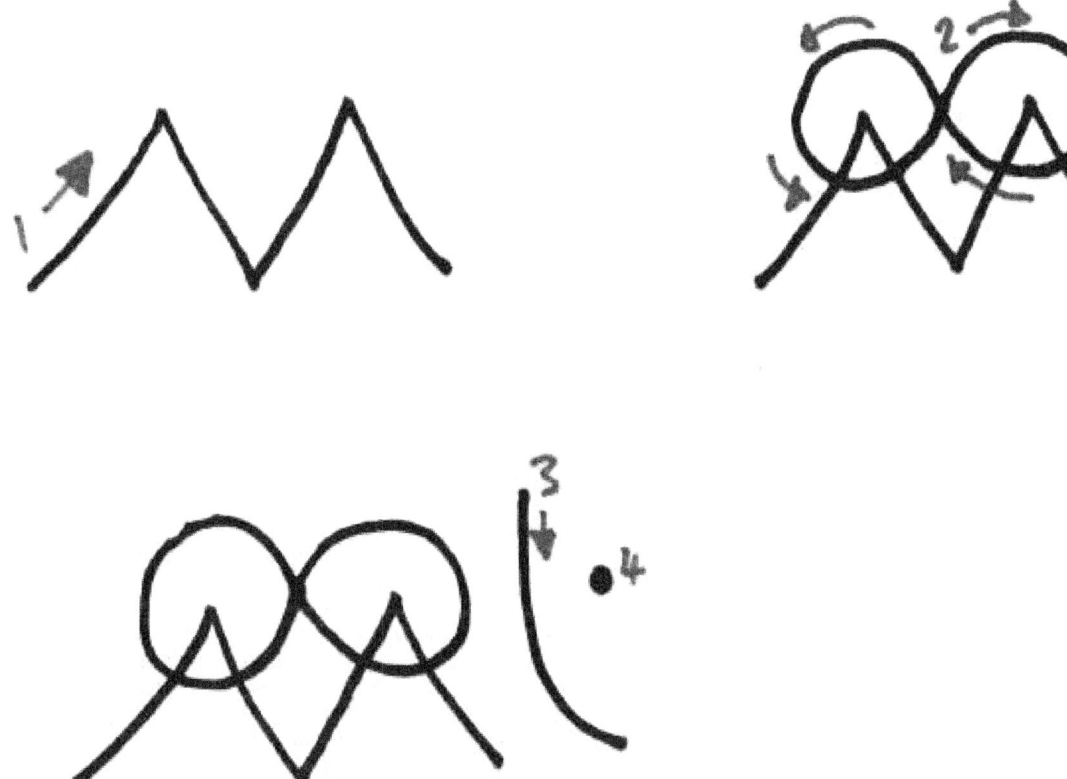

Reproductive Cycle Induced Behavioural Issues

Drawing instructions for a symbol to help with behavioural issues caused by the reproductive cycle

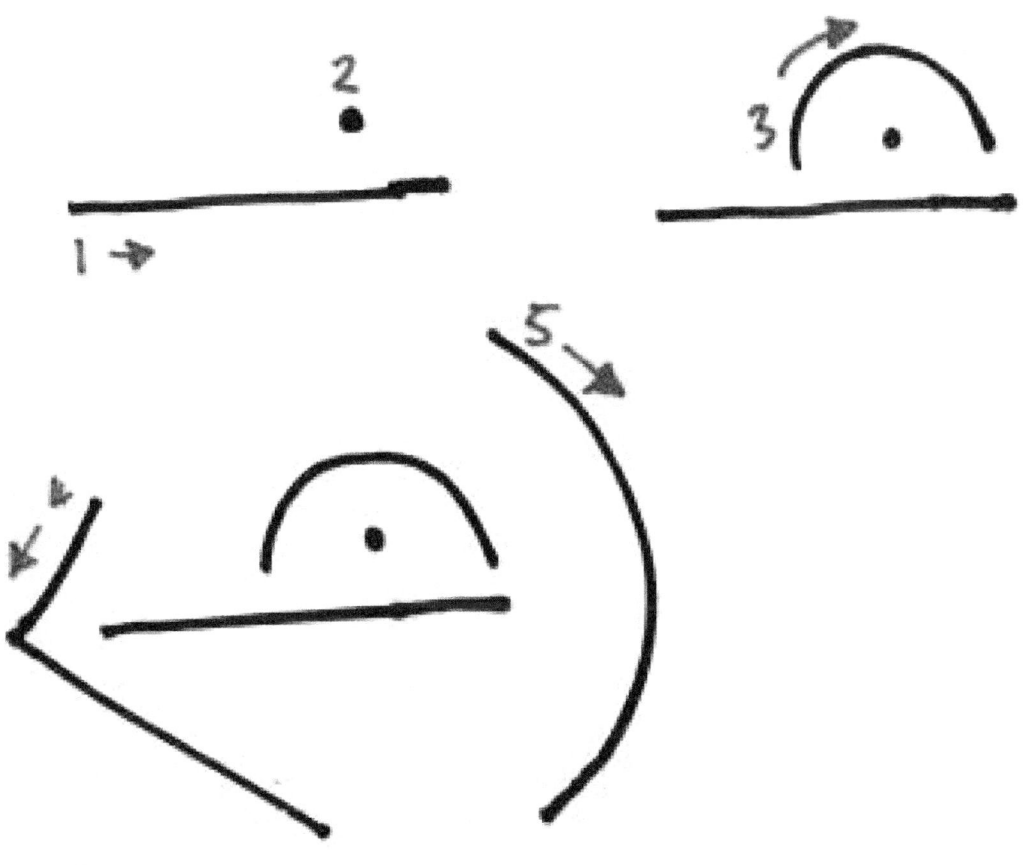

Restlessness

When the animal is unable to rest or relax as a result of anxiety or boredom.

Drawing instructions for a symbol to help with restlessness:

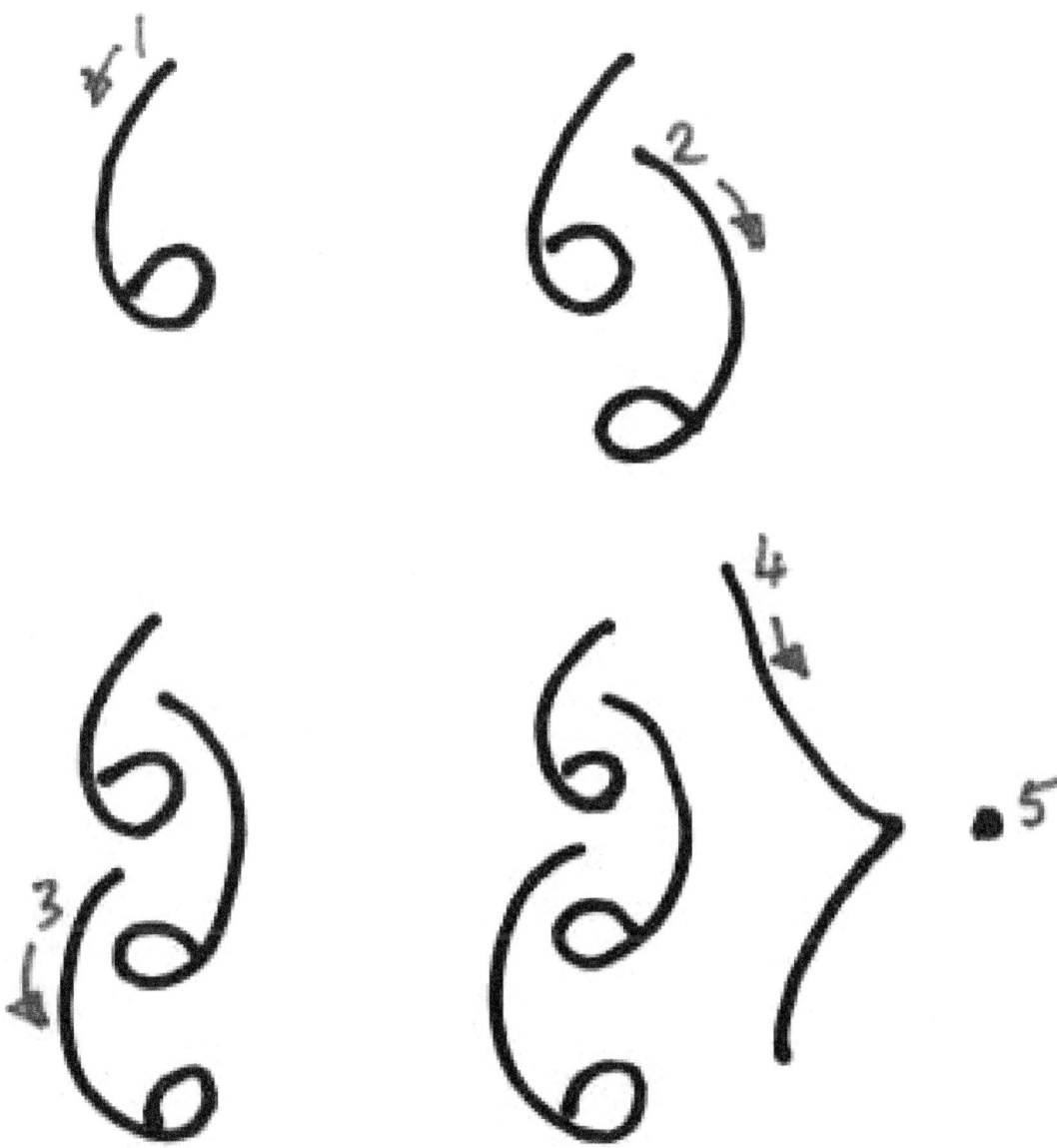

Separation Anxiety

Separation-related behaviour occurs when an animal is left alone or taken away from their regular friends. In many cases, the behaviour is a result of distress.

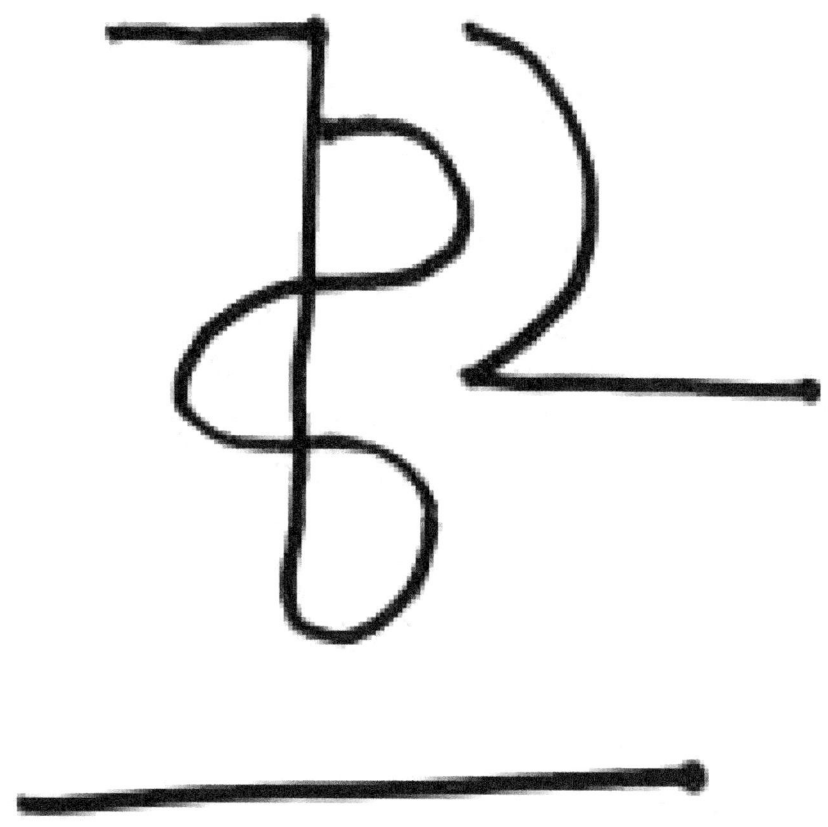

Drawing instructions for a symbol to help with separation anxiety:

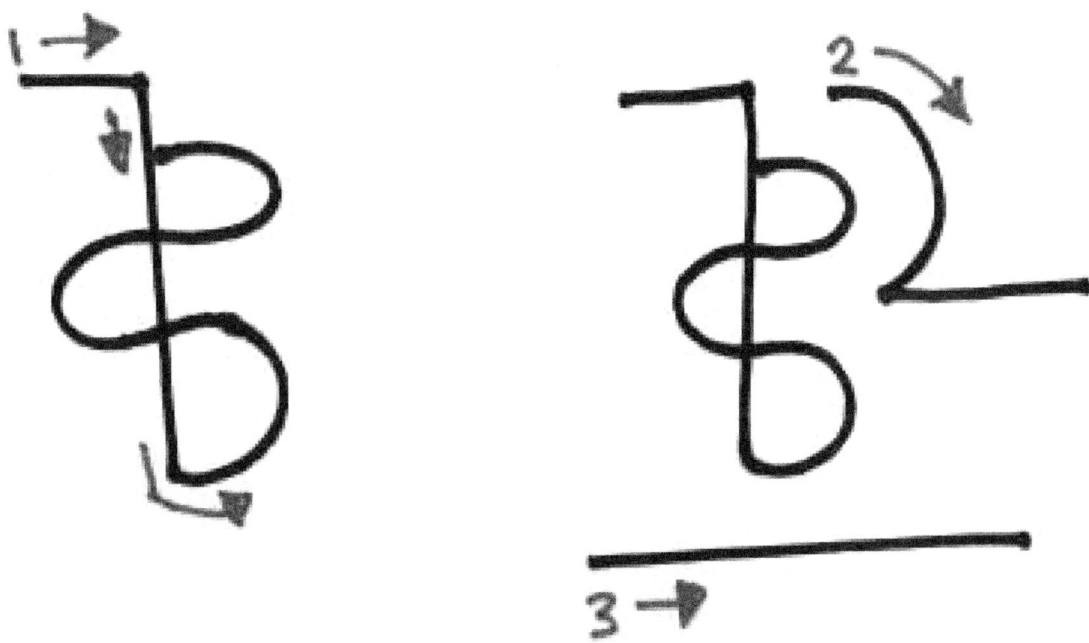

Shoulder Issues

Drawing instructions for a symbol to help with issues of the shoulder:

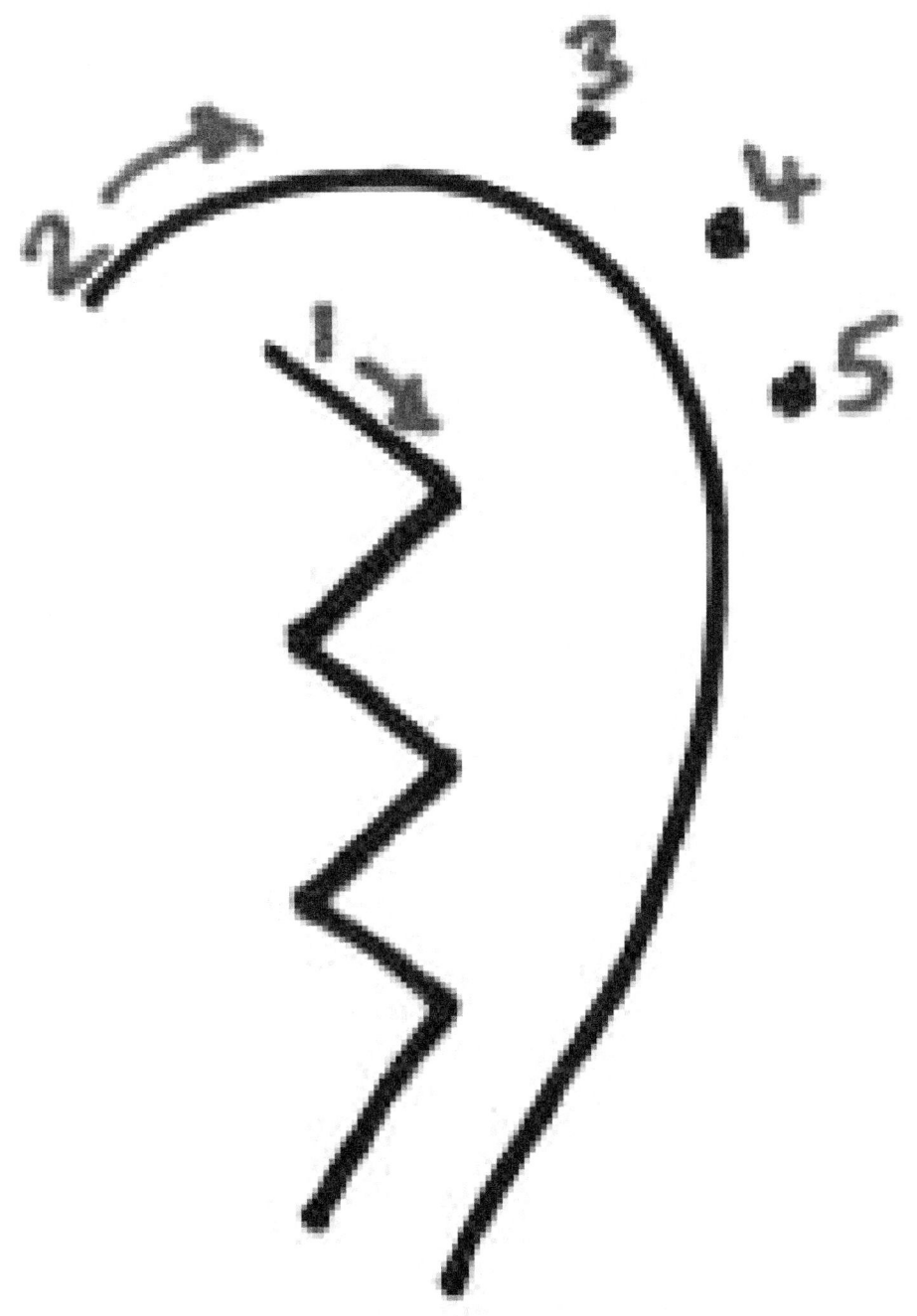

Sickness/ Vomiting

Vomiting is the body's way of clearing out harmful substances from the stomach, or it may be a reaction to a substance that has irritated the gut.

Drawing instructions for a symbol to help with symptoms of sickness/ vomiting

Skin Conditions

Skin disorders vary greatly in symptoms and severity. They can be temporary or permanent and may be painless or painful.

This symbol should be drawn from the centre. You may find that the centre zigzags have more or fewer lines – follow your intuition for the particular animal.

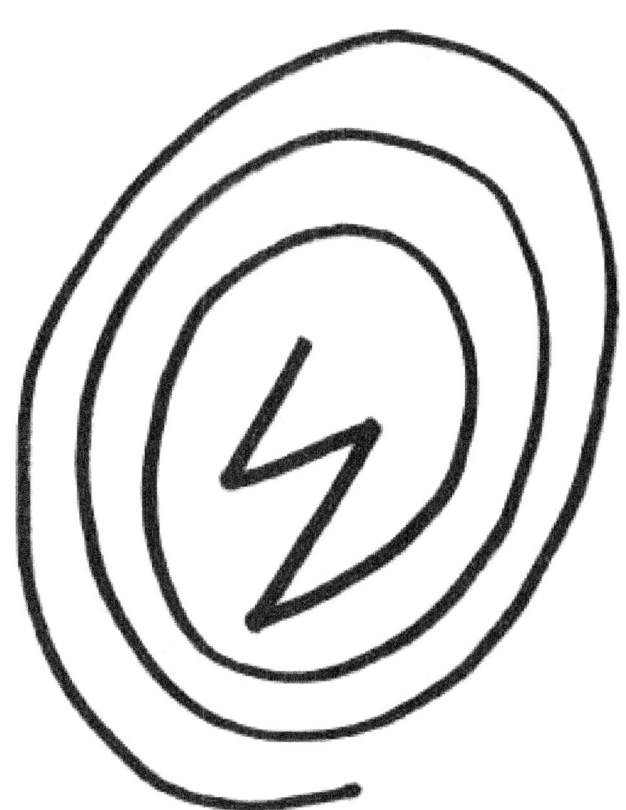

Further ways to draw the symbol to aid with skin conditions

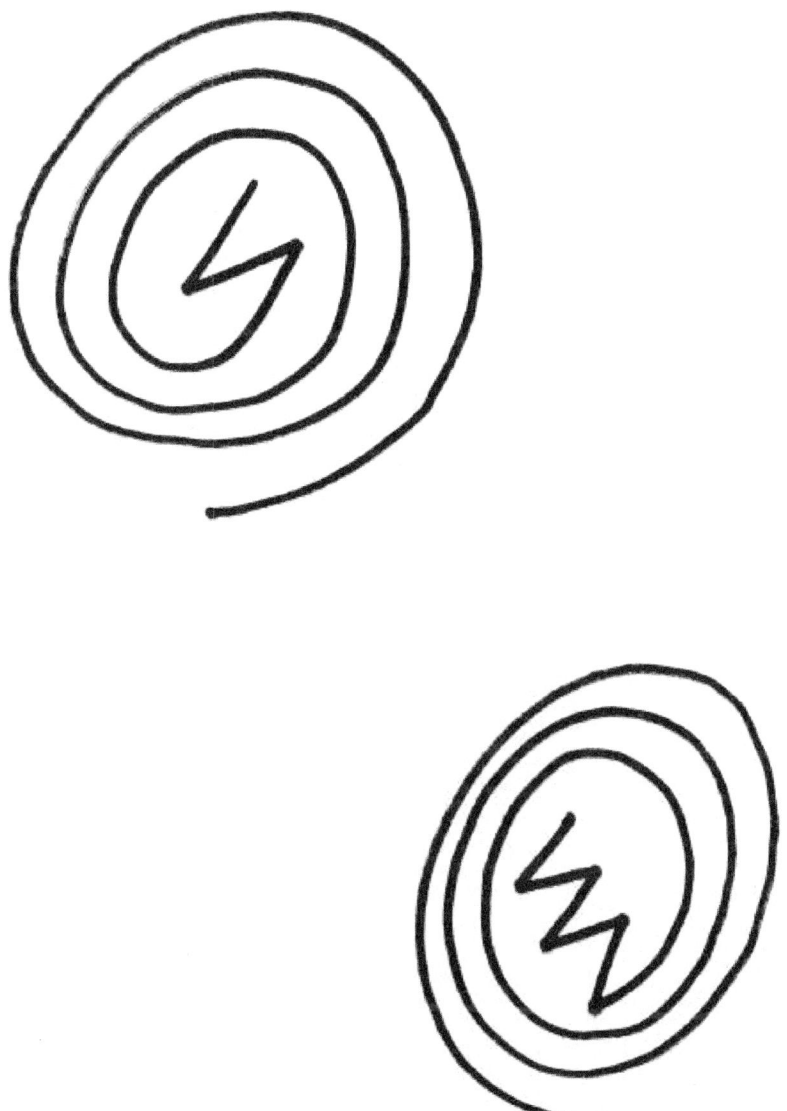

Stomach Ache

A stomach ache is the term often used to refer to cramps or a dull ache in the abdomen.

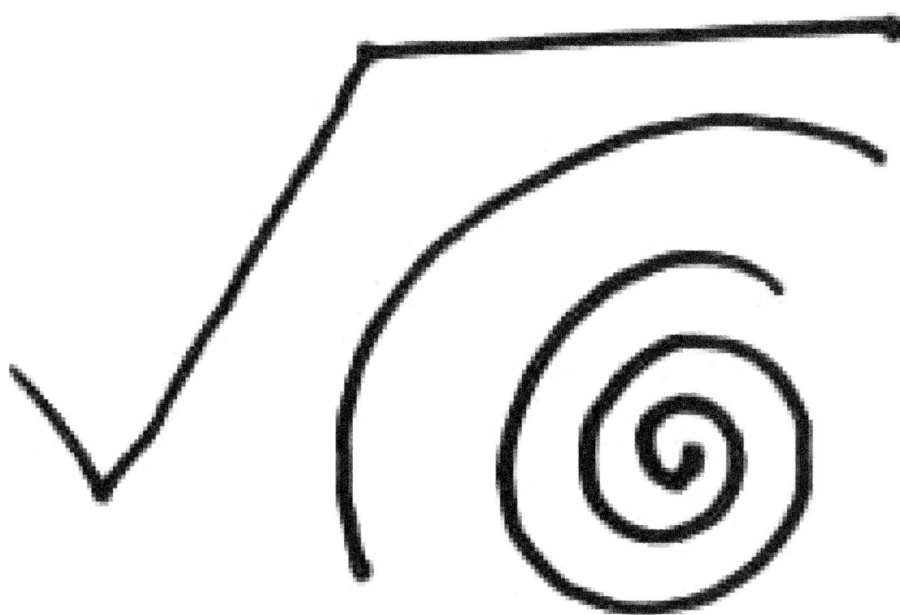

Drawing instructions for a symbol to aid stomach ache:

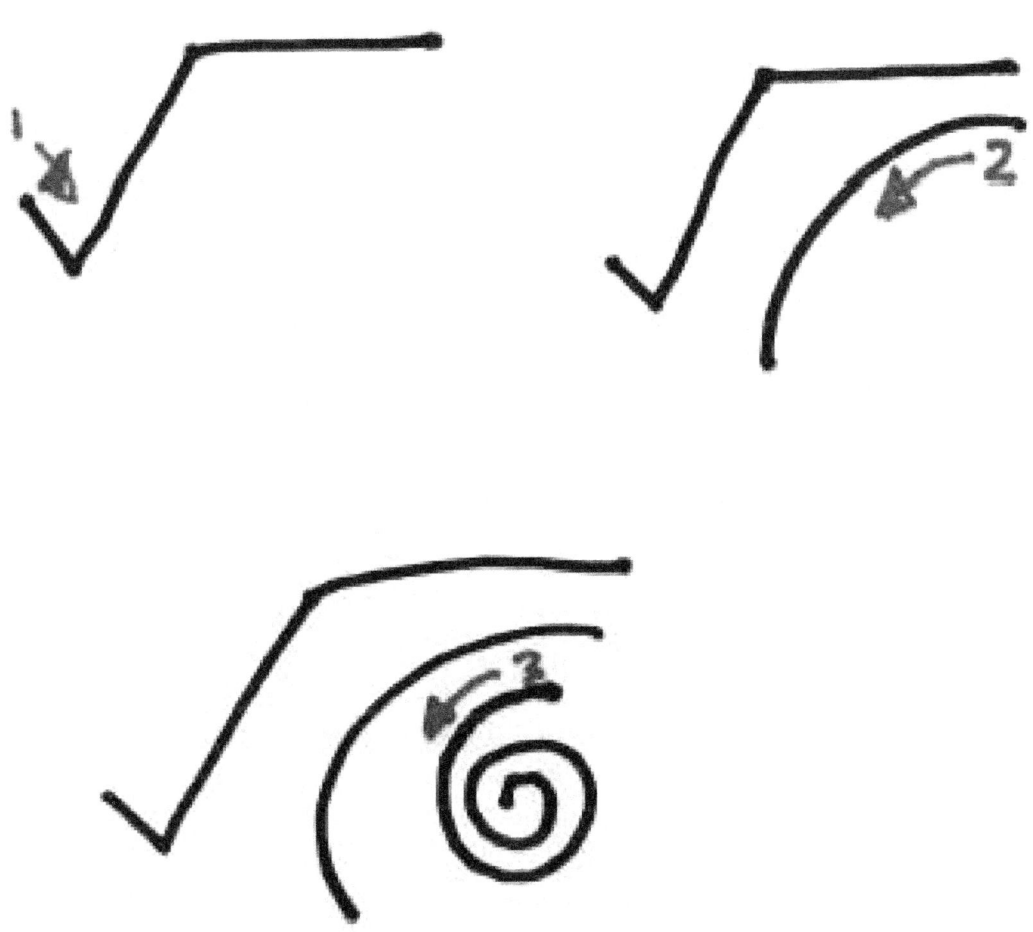

Swelling

Drawing instructions for a symbol to help reduce swelling:

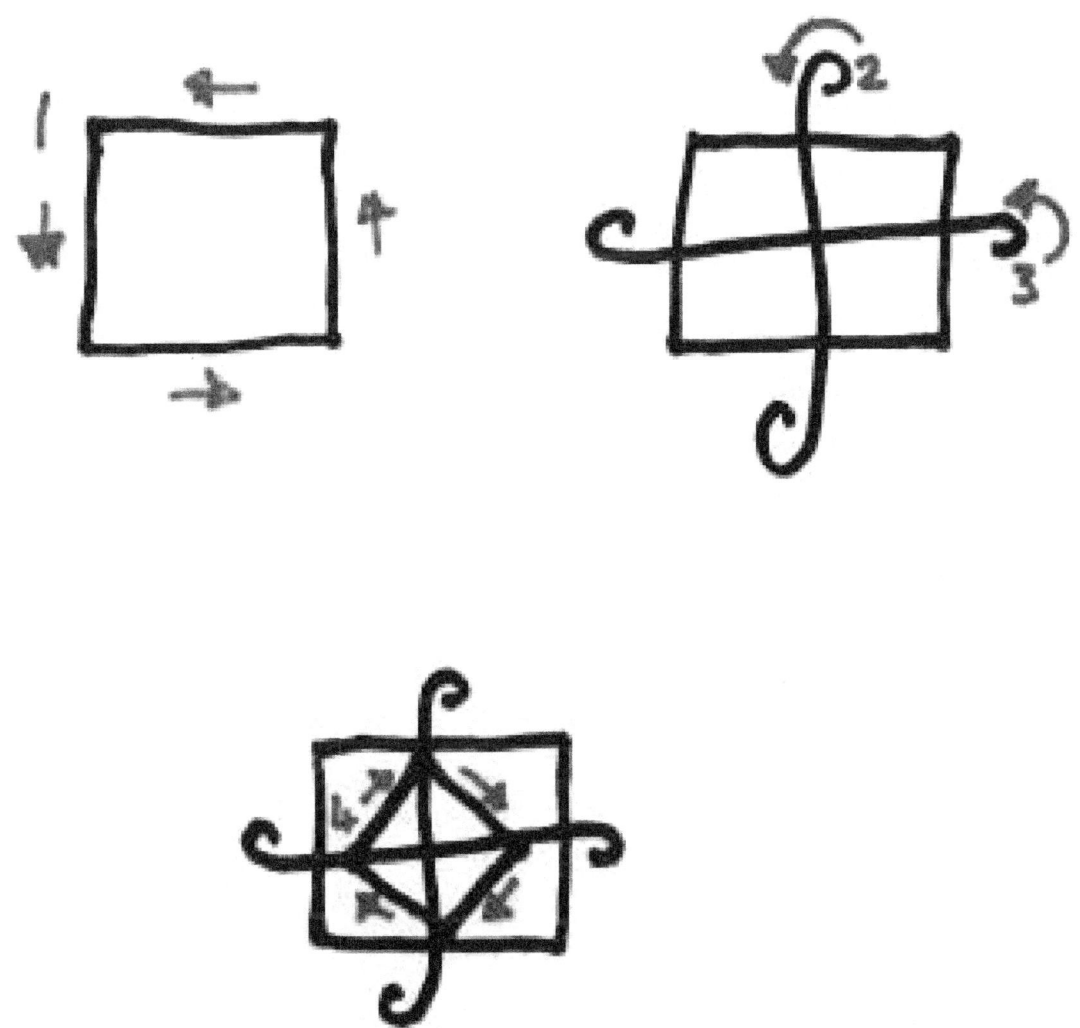

Tail Injury

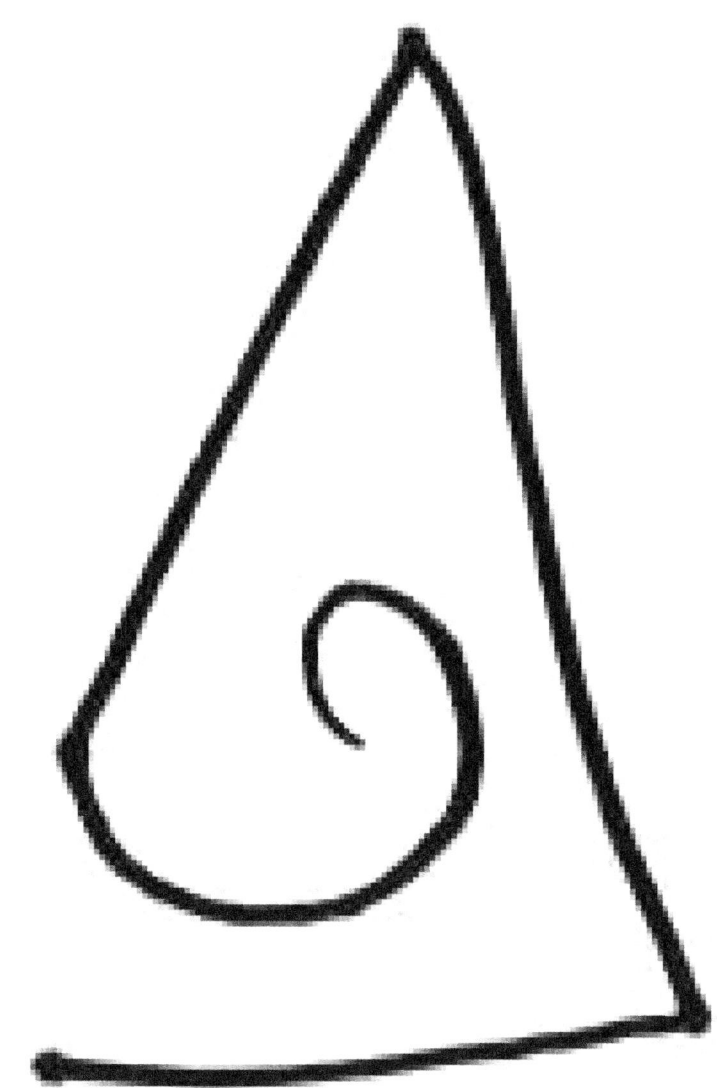

Drawing instructions for a symbol to help with a tail injury

The point of the symbol should be drawn to the base of the tail

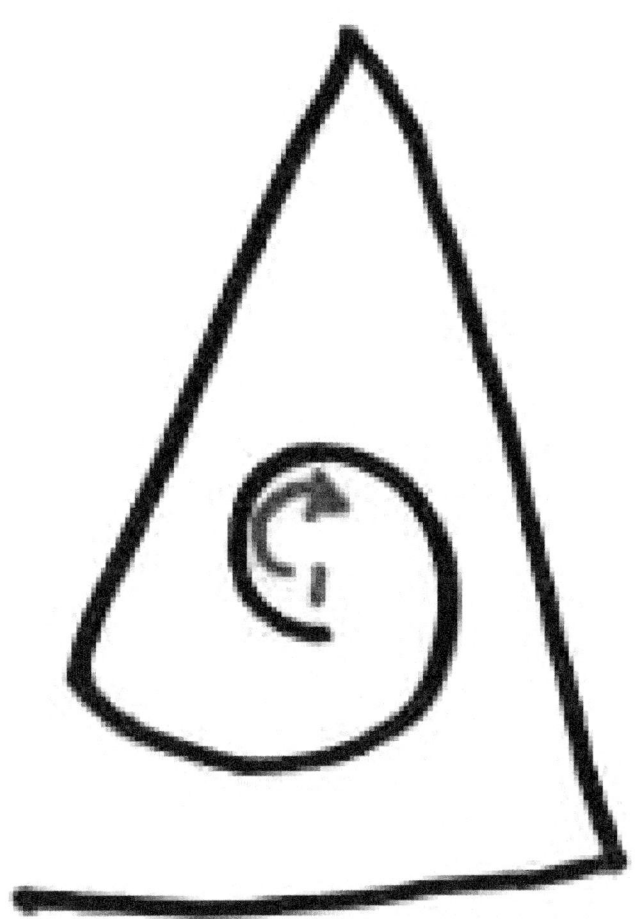

Teeth

Dental problems include tooth erosion, gum infections, cavities and gum diseases. They can cause severe pain and discomfort.

Drawing instructions for symbol to help with tooth problems:

Draw under the jaw if possible

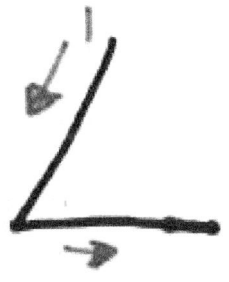 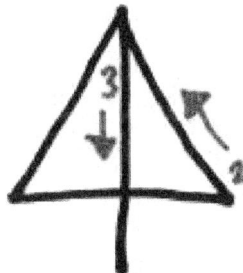 

Tendons/ Ligaments

Common symptoms of tendon and ligament tears are pain and swelling.

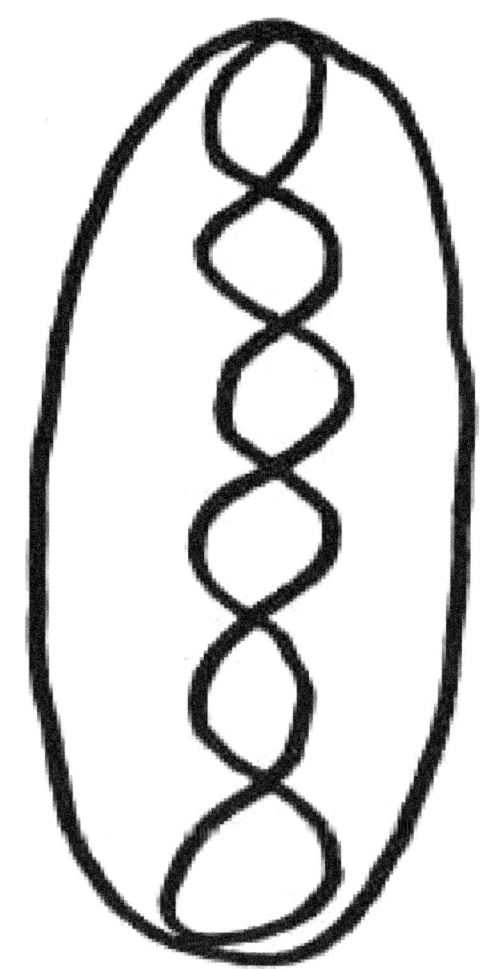

Drawing instruction for a symbol to help with healing tendons and ligaments:

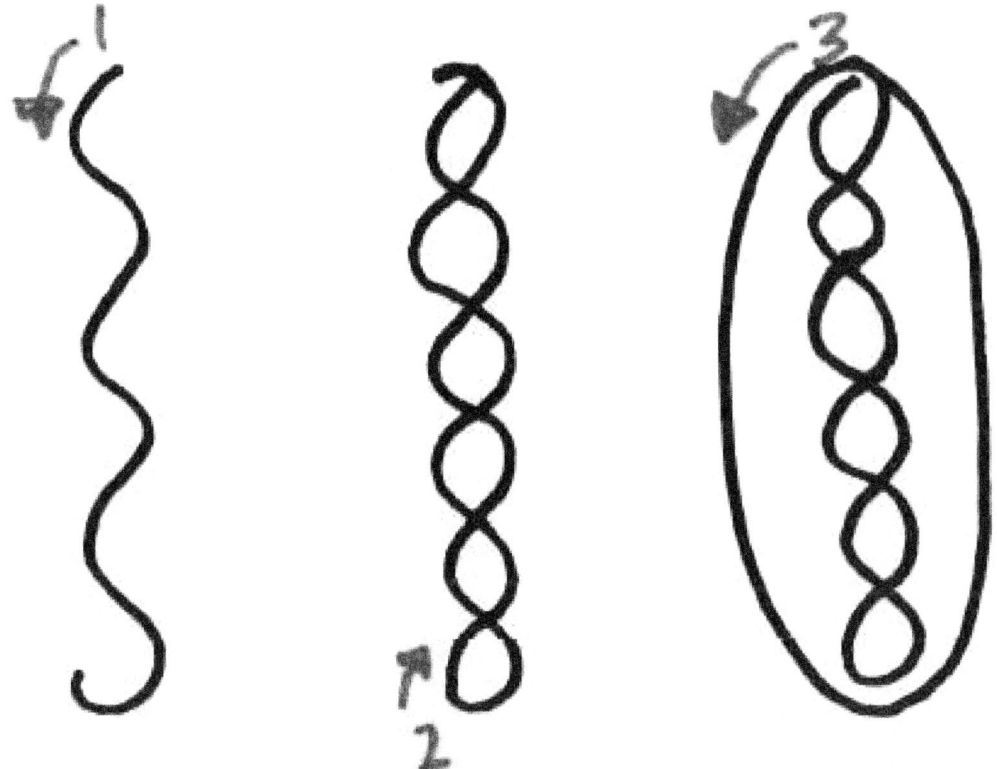

Throat Issues

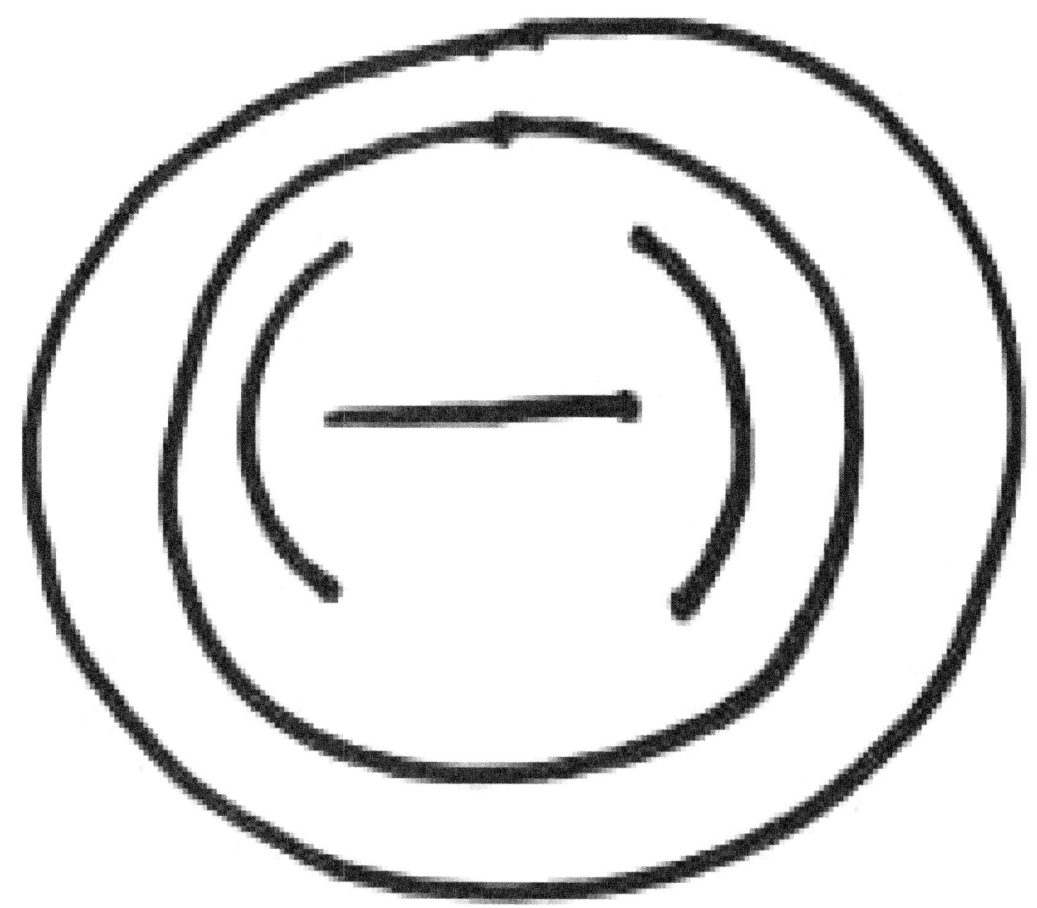

Drawing instructions for a symbol to help with issues of the throat:

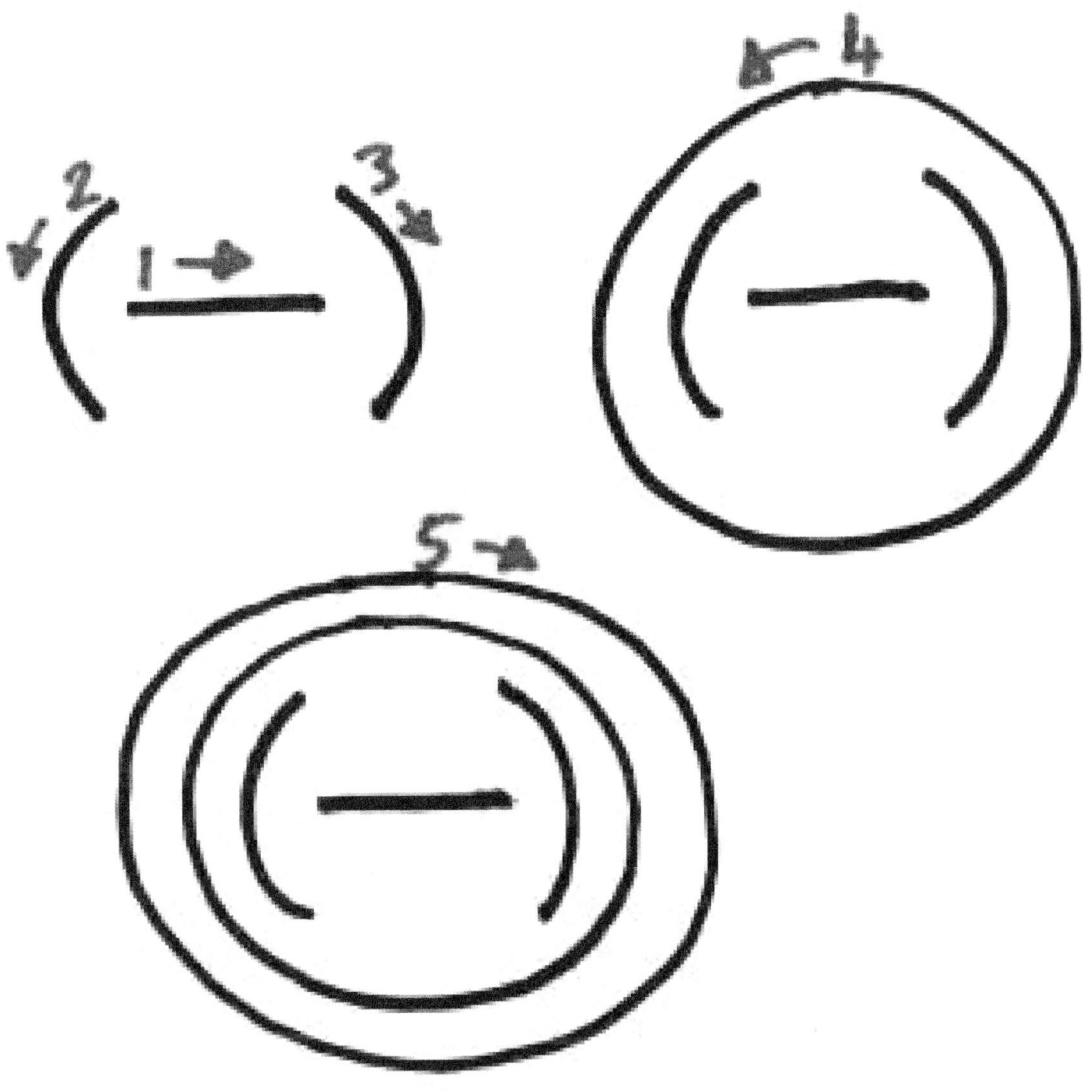

Traumatic Event

A traumatic event is an experience that causes physical, emotional, spiritual, or psychological harm.

Drawing instructions for a symbol to help with dealing with a traumatic event:

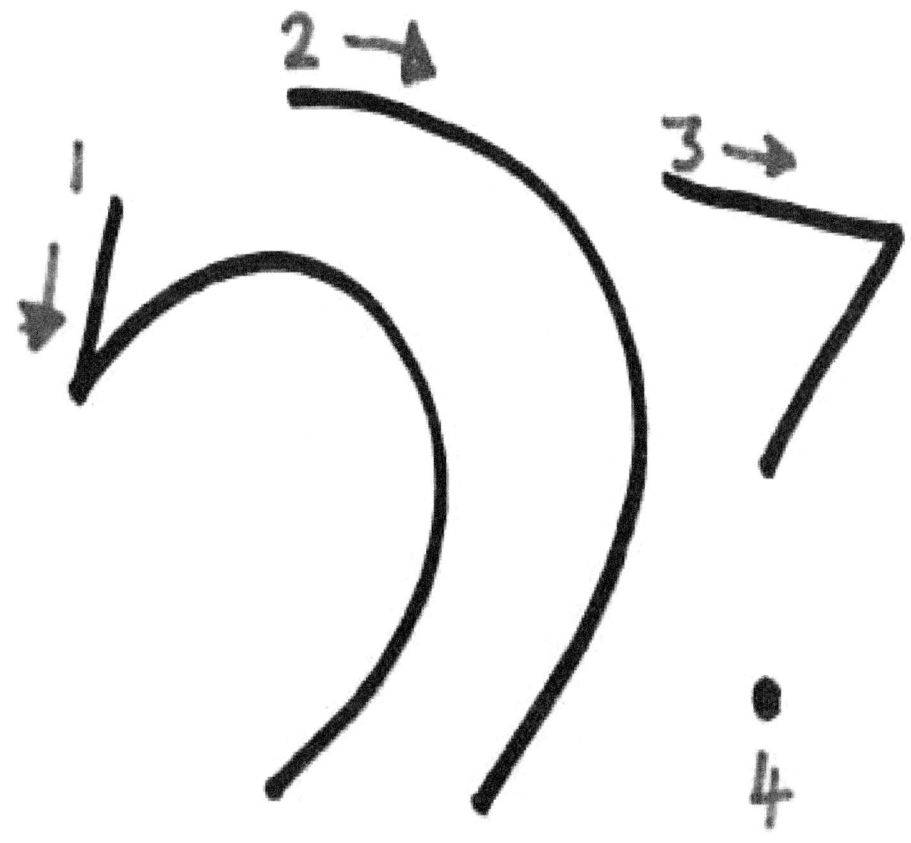

Travelling in vehicles

Drawing instructions for a symbol to help with issues travelling:

Ulcers

Ulcers are sores that are slow to heal or keep returning

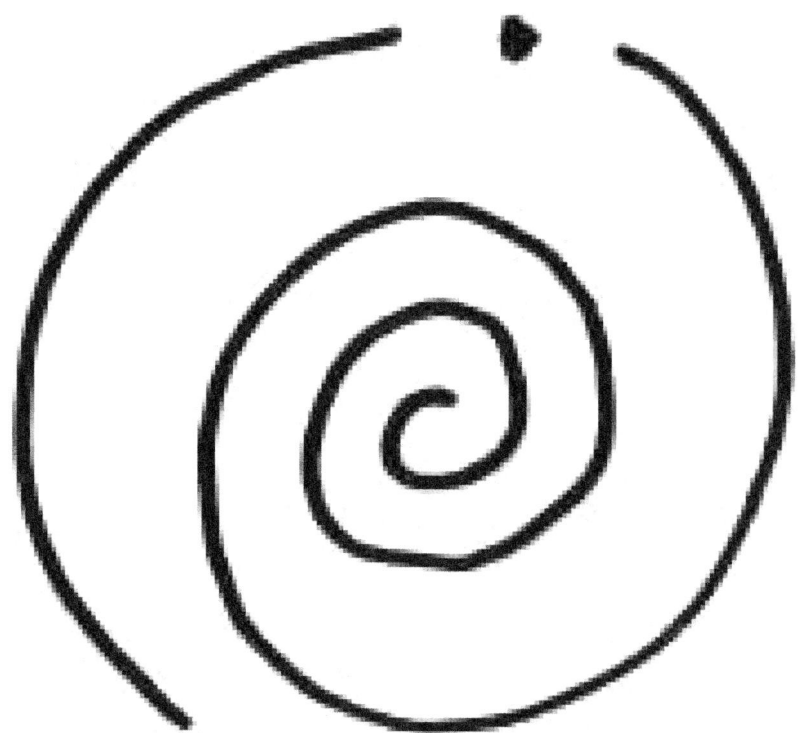

Drawing instructions for symbol to help with ulcers:

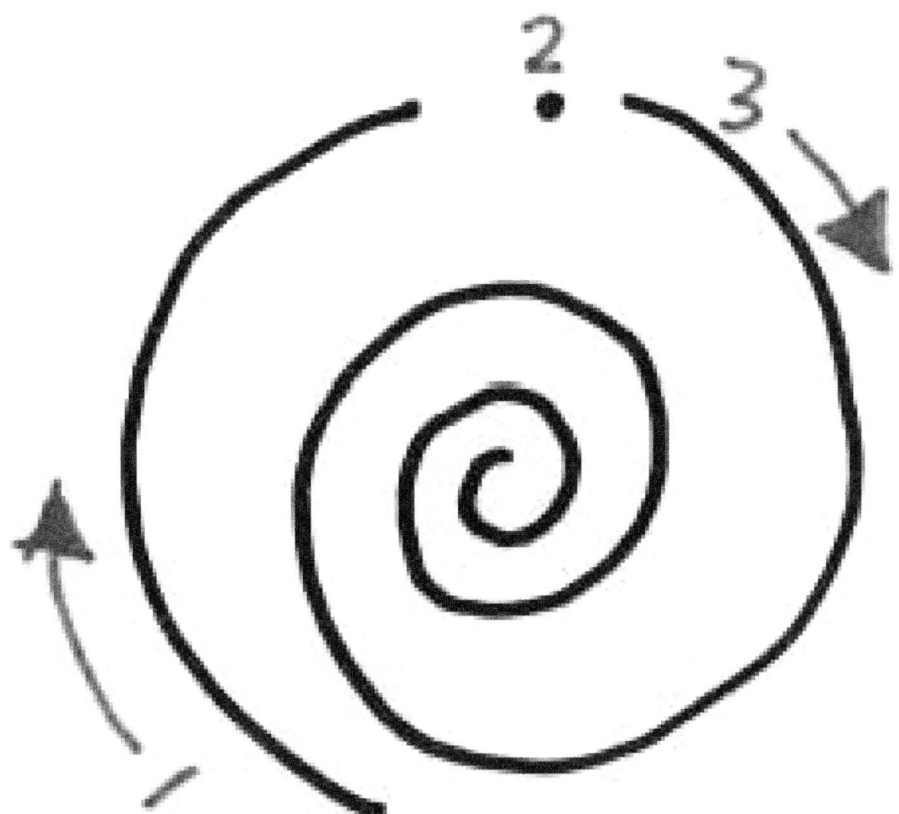

Urinary Tract Infection

A urinary tract infection (UTI) is an infection in any part of the urinary system. The urinary system includes the kidneys, ureters, bladder and urethra

Drawing instructions for a symbol to help with UTI's:

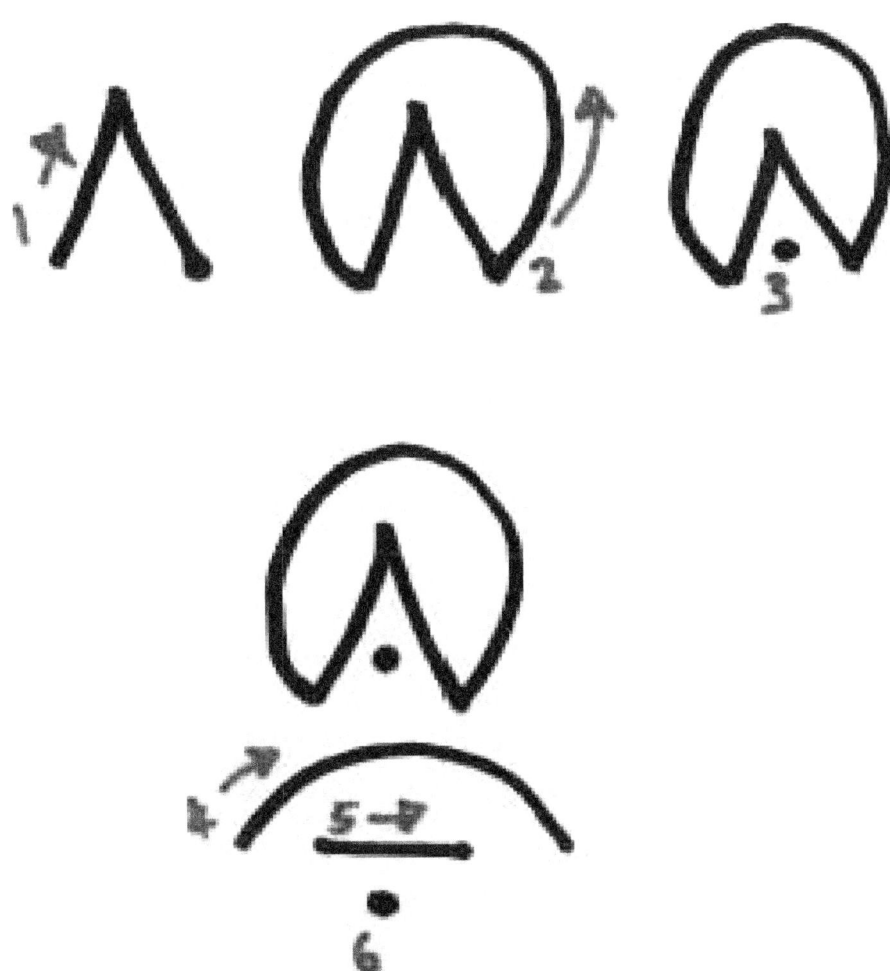

Weaving

Weaving is classed as a stable vice in horses. The horse repetitively sways on his forelegs, shifting his weight back and forth by moving the head and neck side to side. It may also include swaying of the rest of the body and picking up the front legs.

Drawing instructions for a symbol to help with weaving:

Wings

Drawing instructions for a symbol to help with damaged wings or any issue within the wing and its function:

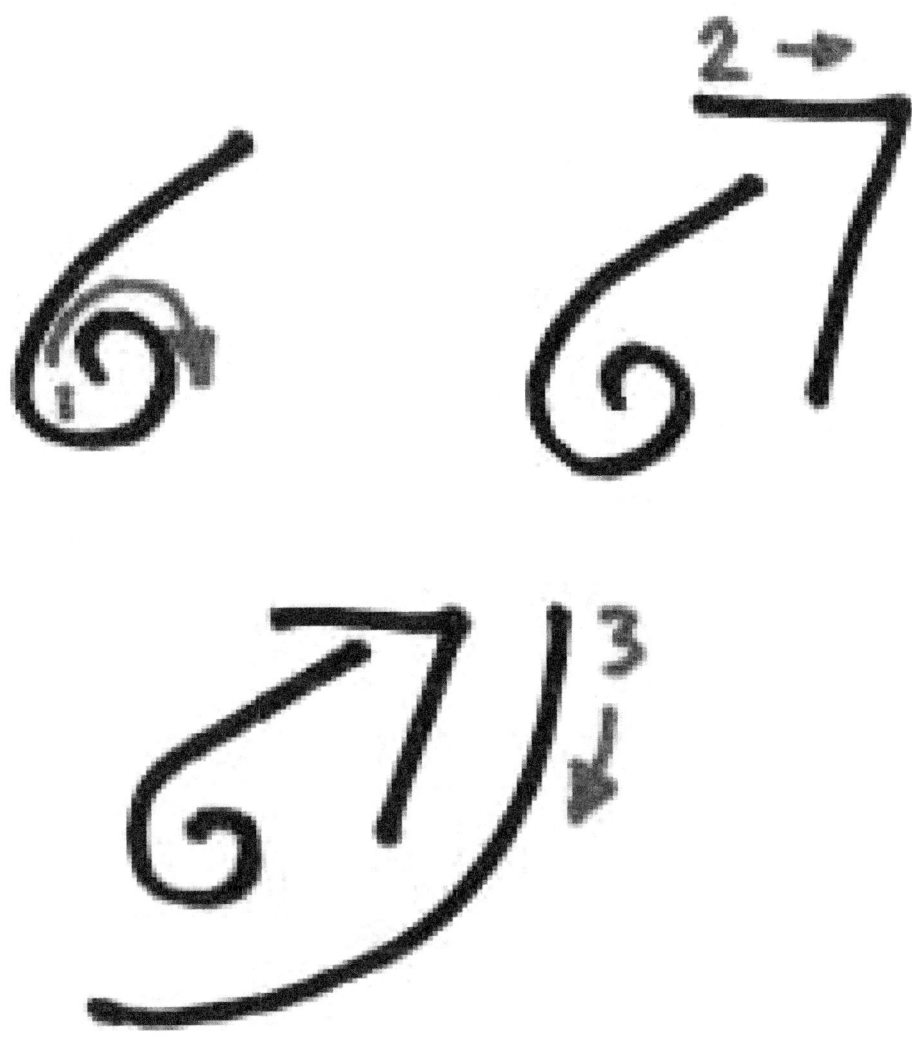

Worm Damage

Weight loss, diarrhoea and colic can all be signs that an animal is suffering from worms.

Drawing instruction for a symbol to help with worm damage:

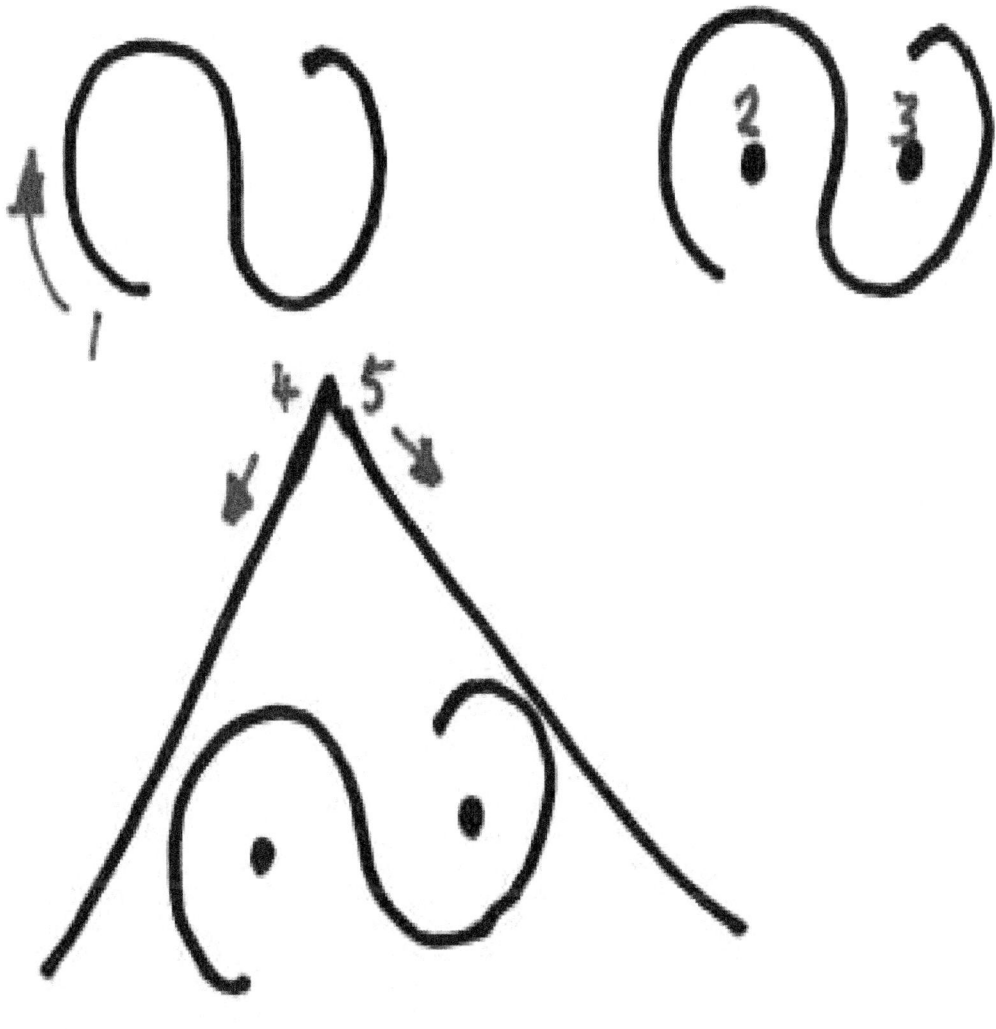

Index

About Sarah

Sarah was born in London, UK. She now lives in South Lincolnshire, where she runs Epona Equine Reiki & Animal Therapy Centre alongside Mistrals Spanish Stud.

Sarah has always had an open attitude towards energy work, healing, herbalism and psychic encounters, with grandparents and great grandparents openly working within these capacities.

In 2007 she was drawn to learn Reiki, which in turn opened many doors for Sarah in the development side of intuitively channelling.

Sarah has worked with many different types of animals over the past 20 years. At home she has Spanish and Rocky Mountain horses, Golden Retrievers, Cocker Spaniels, Guinea Pigs and Pygmy Goats. Barn owls also nest each year on the premises.

This book is dedicated to Janice Brown and Lawrence Pavey, the inspiration behind Sarah's practice.

Printed in Great Britain
by Amazon

40030301R00110